Sa'di

Series editor: Patricia Crone,
Institute for Advanced Study, Princeton

**SELECTION OF TITLES IN THE MAKERS OF
THE MUSLIM WORLD SERIES**

For current information and details of other books in the
series, please visit www.oneworld-publications.com/
subjects/makers-of-muslim-world.htm

MAKERS
of the
MUSLIM
WORLD

Sa'di

The Poet of Life, Love and Compassion

HOMA KATOUZIAN

ONEWORLD
OXFORD

SA'DI

Oneworld Publications
185 Banbury Road
Oxford OX2 7AR
England
www.oneworld-publications.com

ISBN 10: 1–85168–473–5
ISBN 13: 978–1–85168–473–1

Typeset by Sparks, Oxford, UK
Cover and text design by Design Deluxe
Printed and bound in India by Replika Press Pvt. Ltd
on acid-free paper

To the memory of Seyyed Mohammad Ali Jamalzadeh

CONTENTS

PREFACE

They say 'Sa'di speak not so much of her love'
I will, and they will after me in ages to come

I grew up with classical as well as modern Persian literature, and
the first classic I read was Sa'di, whom I have never stopped
studying in the decades since. For a long time, other works and
interests kept me from writing on Sa'di – except for a conference
piece in 1990 – until I decided to do so and wrote on him and his
works in a series of consecutive Persian articles. The results are the
seventeen articles which have been published and the three which
are forthcoming in *Iranshenasi*, listed in this book's Selected Bibliography. Once the series is complete, these articles will be issued by
my Iranian publishers, Nashr-e Markaz, in a single volume.

It will be clear from the contents of this book that it is not just
based on an intimate as well as critical reading of Sa'di's works, but
also on a close familiarity with the entire canon of classical Persian
literature; familiarity with its history, its forms and contents, its
genres and styles, its prosody, and its figures of speech and literary
devices. The opportunity for writing it was offered by the Oneworld
series in which it appears and of which Patricia Crone is general
editor. It pays a debt of honour and hopefully will interest readers
among the lay and the professionals.

HK
St Antony's College and the Oriental Institute
University of Oxford
October 2005

SA'DI, THE CLASSICS AND THE MODERNS

Sa'di is a poet and writer of the seventh century *hijra*, the thir-teenth century of the Christian era, and is one of the greatest classical Persian writers both in prose and poetry. Until the 1940s his *Golestan* was taught to school children as a model of perfect prose, and his *Bustan* was regarded as a guidebook to a moral and virtuous life, much as Aristotle's *Ethics* was regarded in Victorian England. However, not unlike Iranian views in other fields, opinion changed abruptly and drastically in the second half of the twentieth century. Sa'di went out of fashion, and his cult of worship was replaced even more strongly by that of Hafiz. As Jean-Jacques Rousseau might have asked, "How did this change come about?"

Sa'di's impact on later poets and writers has been very great, and certainly until the early twentieth century he was universally regarded as the greatest Persian poet of all time. Sa'di and, fol-lowing him, Hafiz are among the leading stars in the old classical traditions of Persian poetry which began in the tenth and ended in the fifteenth century. From then until the late eighteenth century various new genres and styles emerged, which reached their peak in the so-called Indian style of poetry. This new style, with its emphasis on complex images and metaphors, was refreshing at first and pro-duced at least one outstanding poet comparable to the old classics, i.e. Sa'eb Tabrizi, but time was not on its side. It also suffered from a relative lack of patronage from the ruling Safavid dynasty. Therefore, by the end of the eighteenth century this new style of literature had declined to a level not previously experienced in Persian poetry. This led to a reversion to the old classical styles, a movement which became known as "the literary restoration" and launched the neoclassical styles of the nineteenth century. In this new wave of Persian literature Sa'di cast a long and wide shadow, and virtually all of his works were imitated more or less successfully by poets and writers of the Restoration.

Thus, in the nineteenth century, Sa'di came to be regarded as the leading Persian poet of all time and the greatest hero of Persian literature. In a footnote to his *Hajji Baba of Isfahan*, written in the early nineteenth century, James Morier described Sa'di as "Persia's national poet." Morier was neither a literary critic nor a scholar of Persian literature, and this description undoubtedly reflects what he had heard about Sa'di in Iran.

Of the other classical poets, Hafiz was also greatly admired, and his followers enjoyed reading his poetry while trying to find answers to questions which they would formulate before even opening his book of lyrics, what in Persian is described as *fal-e Hafiz* and is still as popular as ever. Rumi was often described as *Molla-ye Rum*, and was more admired for being a Sufi star than a great poet. It is not surprising, therefore, that readings from his works were largely based on his *Mathnavi-ye Ma'navi* rather than his voluminous divan of lyrics which, although still mystical, are of the highest quality as pure poetry. Ferdowsi was popular for the myths and legends of his *Shahnameh*, which were often recited by the local reciting masters, or *naqqals*, in public places, although he was not normally put at the same level as the first three. Nezami Ganjavi was sometimes added to this list of poets, so that some nineteenth- and twentieth-century classical scholars put him next to Ferdowsi as the fifth member of the galaxy of stars of classical Persian poetry. Khayyam was virtually unknown until his translation by Fitzgerald made him famous in the West and also, in time, in Iran. There was, therefore, no disagreement about the Big Three leading classical poets, while many of the literati added Ferdowsi to make the Big Four, and some included Nezami in the Big Five.

As noted, however, Sa'di topped the list and was regarded as the hero *par excellence* of the history of Persian literature. This was no doubt also the reason why Fath'ali Akhundzadeh (d. 1878), the Azebaijani Iranian who was a subject of the Russian empire and lived in Georgia, launched an attack on Sa'di in his general onslaught on Persian poetry. He was perhaps the first nationalist and modernist Iranian intellectual, and he rejected virtually the whole of post-Islamic Iranian culture, romantically glorified the legacy of ancient Persia, and wished to turn Iran into a Western-European-style country overnight. At the time hardly anyone noticed his vehement campaigns but gradually he came to influence greatly the radical nationalist-modernist intellectuals of the early twentieth century and, through them, the official romantic nationalism and pseudo-modernism of the Pahlavi era.

In his essay *qeretika* (which is a corruption of "critica") Akhundzadeh used the publication of the divan of Sorush-e Isfahani – a notable poet of the time, although by no means a great poet – as a pretext for launching his general attack on Persian poetry. However, it was no accident that he mentioned Sa'di in particular, precisely because of his exalted reputation. Akhundzadeh, like Ahmad Kasravi after him, only excluded Ferdowsi from his general repudiation of Persian poets purely because he had written *Shahnameh*, the book of epics and romances of ancient Persia. In other words, their approval of *Shahnameh* was purely instrumental – for Akhundzadeh, because it glorified ancient Persia; for Kasravi, because it was all about "history," and promoted courage and chivalry as opposed to love and mysticism.[1]

Still, Sa'di remained the hero of Persian poetry well into the twentieth century. In the chaos which gripped Iran after the Constitutional Revolution, and especially after World War I, various diagnoses were being made about the origins of the country's maladies. In 1920 an article appeared entitled "The School of Sa'di" that blamed improper education and lax public morals as the root cause of all the country's problems, and Sa'di in particular for much of them. Once again the reason for identifying Sa'di as the main culprit was his great popularity and the fact that his works, especially *Golestan*, were standard school texts for reading Persian language and literature. A full-scale debate broke out in the journals of the classicist Poet Laureate, Bahar – *Daneshkadeh*, in Tehran – and the modernist Taqi Raf'at – *Tajaddod*, in Tabriz – on the necessity and implications of a "literary revolution" by which they meant a revolution in poetry. In one of his more reasonable arguments Raf'at pointed out that Sa'di's ideas were great for his time but that they were not very helpful for finding solutions to contemporary social problems. The anti-Sa'di campaign lost its momentum once again.[2]

To a considerable extent the 1920s and 1930s were the age of Ferdowsi. Never before had he been regarded with such adulation now that the glorification of ancient Persia had become a part of the official creed. It peaked in the large international Ferdowsi conference in 1934 which was ceremoniously concluded by the opening of his newly reconstructed tomb in Tus. Nevertheless a conference of leading Iranian scholars celebrated Sa'di and his works in 1937 on the occasion of the seven-hundredth anniversary of the publication of *Golestan*. Kasravi who – despite his relative regard for Ferdowsi had strongly disapproved of the conference held in his honour – believed, though not very convincingly, that an equally large international conference had been intended to honour Sa'di but that because of his campaign against it they had settled for the domestic conference.

The conference showed that the traditional cult of worship of Sa'di was as strong as ever. One leading scholar declared that "Sa'di means Persian poetry." Ferdowsi and Hafiz were still thought of highly, but it was considered that Sa'di's poetry belonged to a different order. Another scholar called him "the greatest poet of all poets." Yet another, after mentioning Ferdowsi, Rumi and Hafiz, said "but the collected works of Sa'di is a treasure which knows no value or price." A fourth speaker described him as "the Lord of Word, the greatest appreciation of whom will be to mention his name and say no more." He added that Sa'di was the greatest poet of all time both in East and West. And there was more.[3]

In 1940, Mohammad Ali Foroughi, the prominent scholar, philosopher and politician, published his standard edition of Sa'di's collected works. It contains in its introduction the most elegant, the most eloquent and the most precise version of the traditional adulation of Sa'di and his works. Forughi was a learned scholar, but it is difficult to detect an element of modern criticism in his comments, despite the high standard of his study as a work of scholarship.

The hatred and vilification of Sa'di that began in the 1950s and peaked in the 1970s, and has begun to decline in recent years, must be viewed against the background of this uncritical adulation. This is especially significant as Iranians are not well known for moderate, deliberate and critical approaches in their views and assessments of any subject – literary, political or social. Kasravi's attacks on Sa'di in the early 1940s were not very effective at first, although they must have made an impact when the growing anti-Sa'di campaign began ten years later. Kasravi was opposed to all literature, but especially poetry, and lyrical and mystical poetry in particular, as well as anything that he believed was pessimistic and would loosen morals and discourage the struggle for a better life. Thus Khayyam was also included on his blacklist, and only Ferdowsi was – to some extent – excused. But the main culprits according to Kasravi were the three greatest Persian lyricists: Sa'di, Rumi and Hafiz.[4] His views offended classical scholars to the extent that Poet Laureate Bahar wrote a couple of lampoons against him. But they did indirectly encourage the modernists, though for reasons which were different from his own; although it is hard to believe, they had slowly begun to discover, as they believed, that Persian poetry did not exist before Nima Yushij, the founder of modernist poetry in the twentieth century. The poetry written for a thousand years before him was at best pure versification and at worst worthless nonsense.

It was in the 1950s that the battle lines were drawn between the supporters and opponents of Nima and modernist poetry. Once again there was extremism on both sides and much blood was spilt in the process. By the early 1960s the modernist denunciation of contemporary non-modernist poetry – i.e. poetry written in classical, neo-classical as well as modern (but not modernist) styles – was beginning to turn into the belief, as noted, that Nima was the first ever Persian poet. By the end of that decade this view had become almost universal among modernist-leftist intellectuals, poets and writers. Among the classical greats Sa'di and Ferdowsi became objects of ridicule and denigration.

Still in the 1960s a movement arose that claimed that Hafiz was, if not the greatest, then one of the greatest poets in human history. The cult of Hafiz rose even beyond that of Sa'di before him, while the star of Ferdowsi fell to a nadir because of the belief that he was somehow the ideologue of the contemporary imperial system. But the clear contradiction, of how such a great poet as Hafiz could have emerged in the fourteenth century in a country in which there had been no other poets until the twentieth century, was not explained. Many commentators did not read Hafiz, whom they worshipped, any more than they read Sa'di or Ferdowsi, whom they denied and disparaged. Both sentiments were essentially emotional and uncritical.

There was a debate in the 1940s, when Sa'di was still popular, on whether he or Hafiz was the greatest Persian poet. The Tudeh party critics at the time came down on Sa'di's side because he had written on society and advocated social justice. This attitude, as we saw, changed in the fifties and sixties, and especially in the seventies, which experienced a high tide of irrationalism in Iran, as in other countries, to the extent that young school teachers, virtually all of whom subscribed to one or another leftist ideology, used to turn the page over in the school textbooks whenever they came across a piece by Sa'di. To a considerable extent this was a backlash against the academic classicists' great regard for Sa'di, so that he was increasingly viewed as a symbol of the academic literary establishment in a similar way as Ferdowsi was seen as a symbol of the political establishment. But the rise of leftist irrationalism and emotionalism also played a role, despite the fact that leftist ideologies had been firmly rooted in nineteenth-century rationalist thought.[5] At any rate, literary criticism as distinct from pure scholarship and/or exaltation and vilification has not been a strong point in Iranian culture and history.

The decline of interest in Sa'di among western scholars of the twentieth century was partly due to the decline of classical as opposed to modern studies, and partly the result of Sa'di's unfashionable status among the moderns in Iran. Europe had discovered Sa'di in the seventeenth century when his *Golestan* was translated into

French, German and Latin. In the eighteenth century, translations into English and other western European languages introduced him to the literary public and led to his increasing popularity among the literati and intellectuals. It is not surprising that he was appreciated in the Age of Reason and Enlightenment by its leading figures such as Voltaire, and that Carnot, the French revolutionary leader and organizer of the revolution's defence against foreign invasion, named his son after him, who in turn became a world-famous mathematician. But even Herder, a leading light in the German Counter-Enlightenment movement and philosophical romanticism also thought of Sa'di as "the pleasant teacher of morals."

A recent western study has described Sa'di as a Persian humanist.[6] It especially cites examples of Sa'di's religious toleration as evidence for his humanism, although the requirements of both religious and non-religious types of European humanism go well beyond that, unless the term is employed not in its strict historical sense. Furthermore, as noted, Sa'di had a strong appeal both for the Enlightenment (rationalist) and the Counter-Enlightenment (romantic) thinkers of the eighteenth century. That also puts in balance the view that the decline of European interest in Sa'di and the appeal of Hafiz began with the rise of romanticism in the nineteenth century: Sa'di, as we saw, had also appealed to philosophical romantics. Hafiz's appeal to nineteenth-century thinkers and literati was not so great, with the major exception of Goethe who, however, had shed much of his romanticism by the time he took a strong interest in Hafiz. Hafiz may be described as a romantic only in the broadest of terms, if by romanticism we have in mind the philosophical and literary movement which began in Europe in the eighteenth century and came to maturity in the nineteenth. If, in this broad sense of romanticism, love plays an important role then Sa'di's claim to romanticism should be at least equally as strong as that of Hafiz.

Yet it is true that Sa'di's reputation in Europe was almost completely based on translations of *Golestan* and (much less) *Bustan*, and that – in particular – hardly any attention was paid to him as a great poet of love songs.[7] More translations of *Golestan* appeared in the nineteenth century and Sa'di became a well-known figure among the orientalists. Western interest in Sa'di and his works declined dramatically in the twentieth century, excepting a few critical studies and translations, apart from the general coverage of his works in literary histories and textbooks.[8]

What will happen in the future is not predictable now that Rumi has become popular with the general public in the West, much as Khayyam had done in the late nineteenth century, and that Hafiz still holds much of the attention of western scholars of classical Persian poetry. However that may be, and despite his past fame and fortune, Sa'di is still a largely undiscovered treasure in his own land and the world at large.

LIFE AND WORKS

What is certain about Sa'di's life is that he flourished in the thirteenth century CE (seventh century *hijra*), went to the Nezamiyeh College of Baghdad, travelled wide and lived long. It is clear from his love poetry that he was an ardent lover, and from much of his works that he was not a Sufi although he cherished the ideals of Sufism and admired the legendary classical Sufis. Not much else can be said about his life with the same degree of certainty.

In his introduction to *Bustan*, Sa'di wrote about some of his experiences. Here we learn that he had travelled far and wide and spent time with all manner of people, but for sincerity and generosity he had found nobody like the people of Shiraz. He believed that traditionally travellers, on returning home, normally brought sugar as a gift from Egypt. On his own return home Sa'di wrote:

> If I could not afford to bring sugar
> I can offer words that are even sweeter

Thus he offered *Bustan* as a homecoming present to his fellow citizens. It is clear from the introduction as well as the text that Sa'di had spent many years travelling and seeing the world. In *Golestan* there are many tales and anecdotes which speak of the places the narrator has been to and of the experiences he has had in Baghdad, Mecca, Damascus, Alexandria, Diar Bekr, Hamadan, Isfahan, Balkh, Bamian, even Kashgahr, which is now in China. There is a long tale in *Bustan* of the narrator's visit to Somnath in India, where he has an altercation with and kills a keeper of a Hindu temple. Often, such stories have been believed to be autobiographical, both by Iranian and western scholars such as Mohammad Khaza'eli, John Boyle and Henri Massé. As we shall see below, this is by no means certain and the subject requires a good deal of analysis and speculation.

One thing is certain. Sa'di did go to the Nezamiyeh College in Baghdad. He says clearly in a verse: "I had a scholarship grant at Nezamiyeh." In an anecdote in *Golestan,* he says that, as a youth, he had been under the guidance of Abolfaraj ibn Jawzi, who flourished in the thirteenth century and was a leading scholar as well as the *mohtaseb*, the chief enforcer of religious ethics and duties in Baghdad. That is a good starting point for discussing the dates of Sa'di's birth and death.

BIRTH AND DEATH

For a long time it used to be thought that Sa'di had been born in 1184 CE (580 *hijra*) despite the fact that the traditional date of his death is between 1291 and 1294 (691 and 694), which would mean that he lived for 110 years. Both these dates have been vigorously defended by Khaza'eli and Massé as late as the twentieth century.[9] Their opinion is based on four assumptions. First, Sa'di's mention in *Golestan* of Ibn Jawzi as his guide, who had died in Baghdad in 1200 (597). Second, his statement in *Bustan* that, as a young man, he had travelled with Shahab al-Din Sohravardi. Third, the address in *Bustan* (written in 1257) where he says: "O' you whose age has reached seventy / Were you sleep while it went with the wind?" Last, the story in *Golestan*, in which the narrator says he had visited Kashghar in the year Mohammad Kwarazm-Shah had taken it from Cathay; the date of that event from history is 1213 (610).

The story is a colourful one of a youthful scholar asking the narrator what he knew of "Sa'di's poems." But it is impossible for Sa'di to have been that well known as far east as Kashghar at the age of 29, which is how old he would have been had he been born in 1184. It is also unlikely that Sa'di had ever travelled to the eastern reaches of the Persian speaking world at all: there are no anecdotes in his works in which such important eastern cities as Kerman, Sistan, Nishapur,

Herat and Merv feature. As for Ibn Jawzi, it was discovered in 1932 that the Jawzi Sa'di refers to is the grandson of the elder Jawzi. The younger Jawzi, who died in 1238 (636),[10] had exactly the same name as his grandfather, and he was also a great scholar in Baghdad. There were also two Shahab al-Din Sohravardis. If Sa'di had enjoyed the company of the elder, who was killed in 1189, he would have had to have been born earlier than 1184, whereas Sa'di might well have met the younger Sohravardi, who died in 1234. The verse which mentions the age of seventy is clearly a general, not personal address, for in a following verse Sa'di adds, "Now that you have lost fifty years/Try to appreciate the remaining five days."[11]

Therefore Sa'di could well have been born at the beginning of the thirteenth century. In the introduction to *Golestan*, in a verse clearly addressed to himself, Sa'di says, "You who have passed fifty years and are still not awake" (i.e. not awakened to the transience of life and the need to repent). He wrote *Golestan* in 1258 (656). This line implies that he was fifty years old or more at the time, and so was born in 1208 or a little earlier. On the other hand, he says in a little known *qasideh*, which he wrote in the 1250s, that he had left home for foreign lands when the Mongols had come to his homeland, Fars. We know from history that this happened in 1225 (622). Thus he was seventeen or more when he went to Baghdad, and this is consistent with the above account that, when young, he fell under the guidance of the younger Jawzi.

To sum up, Sa'di is very likely to have been born in 1208 or a couple of years earlier. The date of his death, as noted, has been consistently stated to have been between 1291 and 1294, which would mean that he lived for a maximum of eighty-six years, a long – but not impossible – life for that time. Still, these dates may or may not be correct. We lose chronological sight of Sa'di around 1281 (680).

The great viziers, and brothers, Shams al-Din and Ata-Malek Joveini both met a tragic death in the early 1280s. They were also men of great learning, the former being a poet, on one of whose poems a well-known *ghazal* by Hafiz is based; the latter is the author of *Tarikh-e Jahangosha*. Sa'di was a friend of both, and wrote a number of eulogies for them, yet conspicuously there is no elegy in his works for either of them, especially given the manner of their fall and demise. Did Sa'di also die in the early 1280s, when he was in his 70s?

As noted, Sa'di presented *Bustan* to his fellow citizens as a gift on his return to Shiraz. In the introduction to that book he has recorded the date of its publication as 1257 (655):

> It was six hundred and fifty five years after *hijra*
> When pearls filled up this famous treasure

He must therefore have returned home in the early to mid-1250s. Given that, as mentioned above, he had left Shiraz in the 1220s, he had therefore spent thirty years of his life travelling abroad, learning, teaching and observing. The fact that he returned to Shiraz in the 1250s is no evidence that he had been away continuously for thirty years; he might have come and gone several times between the 1220s and the 1250s. However, there is evidence from elsewhere. He says clearly in the *qasideh* mentioned above not only that he had left about 1225 (622) when Sa'd ibn Zangi was (the Solghorid) ruler in Fars, but that he returned when his son Abubakr ibn Sa'd was ruler, and the horrors of the (first) Mongol invasion had subsided, when "the claws of the wolves had gone blunt" and "the leopards had abandoned the ways of leopards."[12]

SA'DI'S POETICAL SIGNATURE

At some stage the poet's pen name and poetical signature became "Sa'di". Up until now there has been a virtual consensus of scholarly opinion that he took this from the name of his young patron Sa'd, son of Abubakr ibn Sa'd, the heir apparent, especially as Mohammad Qazvini argued it at length in the 1930s. As we have seen, Sa'di left Shiraz under the younger Sa'd's grandfather, and returned under his father Abubakr, when he was heir apparent. As it happened the younger Sa'd died young while travelling, shortly after the death of his father in 1260 (658).

Sa'di wrote two moving elegies for the sudden and unexpected death of his patron. Two years earlier he had expressed a strong wish in the introduction to *Golestan* that Sa'd would "appreciate" that book, and had more or less presented it to him: "More especially since its majestic preamble/Is in the name of Sa'd ibn Abubakr son of Sa'd ibn Zangi."

But did he take his poetical name (*takhallos*) from this Sa'd, or from his grandfather? Notwithstanding the traditional consensus to the contrary, the evidence suggests that he took it from the grandfather. First, when Sa'di left Shiraz, between seventeen and twenty years of age, the elder Sa'd, as we have seen, was ruler of Fars. A poet of Sa'di's calibre must have begun his literary career at a very young age and have produced publicly presentable work by the age of fifteen, the age at which, both legally and socially, men were regarded as adults in this period. He is therefore likely to have read poems at the court and taken his *takhallos* from Sa'd ibn Zangi.

Second, he has a wealth of love poetry that reflects a rich experience of loving, and virtually all of which bears the poetical name Sa'di. It is extremely difficult to imagine that all these love poems were written after he was fifty. Lastly, he has a *qasideh*, written almost on his arrival back in Shiraz, which begins: "Sa'di left on foot and returned on his head." This shows that he already had the poetical name Sa'di when he returned to Shiraz.

SA'DI'S TRAVELS

The question of Sa'di's travels is a good deal more vexed and less clear-cut than many scholars, especially Khaza'eli, Massé and Boyle, have presumed.[13] The problem arises from the belief that every anecdote in *Golestan* (and the few in *Bustan*) which is related by the first person singular pronoun must refer to Sa'di himself. Indeed, Khaza'eli believes that otherwise the great sheikh would have to be declared a wanton liar. In fact many of them are likely to be fiction told by the story's narrator in the first person. Occasionally, confusions arise from misinterpretation. For example, there is a story in verse in *Bustan*'s chapter three, "On Love, Intoxication and Ecstasy," well worth telling, where the narrator says that he and a Sufi Guide (*pir*) reached the sea "in the land of *maghreb*." He had ten drachmas and was allowed to board the ship, but the *pir* was left since he did not have any money. As the *pir* could not travel on the boat, he spread his prayer mat and sailed on it.

> By chance I and a *pir* from Fariab
> Reached water in the land of *maghreb*
> I had ten drachmas and they took
> Me on board, but left him to look...
> I wept, being unhappy for my friend
> He laughed aloud at my tears and said
> Stop being sad for me in friendship
> I will be brought by He who brings the ship
> He spread his prayer mat on sea, seeming
> It was a hallucination or I was dreaming
> All night long in astonishment I did not sleep
> In the morning he said, looking at me deep
> You came on a piece of wood, I, on foot
> God brought me, and you were brought by the boat
> [*Kolliyat*, p. 289.]

Walking on water has been reported not just for Christ but also for many saints and sages in the Middle East. In Iranian mythology, Fereydun and Key Khosraw after him, both of whom were blessed with Divine Grace, rode through vast and turbulent rivers.

Even putting that aside, it would not prove that Sa'di had travelled as far west as Morocco, as the above-mentioned authors believe on the strength of the fact that the story happens in "*maghreb*." Here as elsewhere "*maghreb*" is a general term which Sa'di uses for the west, and especially the lands around the eastern Mediterranean. For example, in the third chapter of *Golestan*, "On the Virtues of Contentment," he tells the story of the very rich merchant who did not sleep all night in the Isle of Kish (in the Persian Gulf). In the story, the merchant gives the narrator a list of all that he possessed and tells him about his incredible travel plans for buying and selling goods until, when he had finished, he would just retire to a shop and stop travelling. When at last the merchant tires of talking and asks the narrator to say something, Sa'di says:

> Have you heard that once a merchant
> Fell in a desert off his riding beast [?]
> 'The greedy eyes of the materialist'
> He said 'will either contentment fill
> Or the dust of his grave still'
> [*Kolliyat*, p. 109.]

While boasting about his travel plans, the merchant "sometimes said that 'I long for Alexandria, which is beneficent', and then said, 'No, since the Sea of *Maghreb* is turbulent'." It is clear from these references that "*maghreb*" refers to the eastern Mediterranean, not Morocco. In a story in the second chapter of *Golestan*, "On the Morals of Dervishes," the tale is told of a sage who once fell in a brook in Damascus and almost drowned. A disciple of the sage said that he had once seen him walk on water in "the Sea of *Maghreb*," and wondered at how he was now about to drown in a brook. The sage replied indirectly that saints and sages are not always in a state of ecstasy and elation. Once again "*maghreb*" here clearly refers to the eastern Mediterranean, not Morocco.

As noted, the story of Sa'di's presence in 1213 (610) in Kashghar is bound to be fictional for the reasons mentioned above. He tells a story in chapter seven of *Golestan*, "On the Effects of Education," of travelling in Balkh and Bamian (in present-day Afghanistan) with a guard who was very strong but lacked experience. He kept boasting about his ability, but as soon as two highwaymen appeared he began to tremble, so that they had to hand over their possessions to save their lives. These are the only two stories about travelling in eastern Persia and Persian-speaking lands, whereas there are many about travelling in the west, in both Persian and Arab regions. Besides, as previously noted, there are no stories involving places such as Nishapur, Kerman and Herat, famous Persian cities en route to the East. It therefore seems likely that both the above stories are fictitious and that Sa'di never travelled to the eastern lands.

The story of travelling to, and the killing in, Somnath is so fantastic that it makes one wonder how it came to be believed by so many – Boyle and Massé among them – to be an historical account of personal experiences. The narrator travels to Somnath – a sacred city of the Hindus, well known in the Persian world for the raids and plunders of Mahmud of Ghazna two centuries earlier – and hides in the main Hindu temple. While hiding, he discovers that a keeper of the temple pulls a rope from behind a screen each time the "ivory idol" appears to raise its hands to the great awe and wonder of the worshippers. The keeper discovers the narrator and realizes that he has discovered his secret. A struggle follows and the narrator kills him. Related in verse in chapter eight of *Bustan*, "On Gratitude for Well-being," it is one of the weakest stories of that book from an artistic and technical point of view. It is long-winded, shallow in content and conclusion, and of limited worth only for some of its imagery. He concludes from this long and boring tale that human action is guided by God, just as the idol's hands were pulled up by the temple priest. It is almost certainly fictitious.

Where did Sa'di really travel to, then? The answer to that question cannot be known with a high degree of certainty, but may be surmised from his works. We can be certain he went to Baghdad because of his scholarship at the Nezamiyeh College, and Damascus and Mecca are very likely also to have been visited. There is no reason for believing Jami, Dawlat-shah Samarqandi and those who have repeated their claim that he went on pilgrimage to Mecca on foot fourteen times, although there is enough evidence in his works to suggest that he almost certainly did go to Mecca, and probably more than once. There is also evidence that he spent time in Syria, especially in Damascus, which was a leading Islamic city and place of learning at the time. He is likely to have travelled in Palestine and, with less likelihood, visited Egypt, including Alexandria. On his way back home it is probable that he travelled through Diar Bekr, which he mentions in his stories, but not Anatolia, which he does not mention. If he went to Hamadan and Isfahan, this cannot be borne out by the stories his narrators relate to them, they being obviously fictitious: in one case the story is anachronistic, and in the other, fantas-

tic. It is not unlikely that he went to Azerbaijan and met the brothers
Joveini mentioned above, the two ministers of the Mongol emperor,
Abaqa. This is not mentioned in the tales of *Golestan* and *Bustan,* but
is found in a source quoted from him in the early manuscripts of his
works, in a language and idiom which seem authentic.[14]

ESCAPE FROM SCHOOL?

Damascus and Syria feature more in the stories told in the first
person singular even than Baghdad. There are two stories about his
experiences in Syria that, even if wholly or partly made up, shed light
on his intellectual and spiritual development. They help to explain a
question about his life which seldom if ever has been asked, namely,
why this sheikh and doctor of a particularly orthodox college, the
most prestigious in its part of the world, gave up academic life to
become a poet and writer. He says in chapter two of *Golestan* that
he was once lecturing at the University (*Jame'*) of Baalbek (now in
Lebanon) and felt that his audience was unenlightened and void of
intellectual and spiritual depth. He felt as if he was "educating beasts
and selling mirrors in the district of the blind." Yet he continued
interpreting the Qor'anic verse in which God is quoted as saying:
"And we are closer to him [i.e. human being] than his jugular vein."
He puts this in Persian verse:

> My Friend is closer to me than me
> And, strange to say, I am far from Him
> What shall I do, whom shall I tell that He
> Is beside me and I am afar from Him?

These words draw a response, not from his audience but from an
enlightened passer-by, and it was his passionate reaction that shook
the others up to come to their senses.[15]

He could scarcely have been more critical of the formal scholastic
environment, especially as he compares it with the presence of mind
of a non-scholastic person. In the same chapter of *Golestan* he tells a
colourful story that may have more significance than readily meets

the eye. He says he had grown weary of the company of his friends in Damascus and left through the desert of Jerusalem, where he lived in the company of animals until the Franks took him prisoner and put him to hard labour in Tripoli. An important man from Aleppo who knew him bought him from the Franks for ten dinars, and gave him his daughter's hand in marriage for a marriage portion of a hundred dinars. The marriage was not successful. Once, the woman taunted him by recalling that her father had bought him back from the Franks. He replied: "Yes ... he released me from Frankish bondage for ten dinars and got me bonded to you for a hundred."[16]

Sa'di might have had some or all of the experience related in the above story, or it may be wholly or partly fictional. Either way it is significant that the narrator who, even if not Sa'di, is doubtless a distinguished scholar felt so alienated from his friends and colleagues in Damascus that he went into the desert without the slightest prospects and with the risk of falling into the hands of the Franks. Once again we observe a case of alienation from the formal scholastic circles. The reader may be reminded of the case of Abu Hamed Ghazali who, two centuries earlier, secretly fled the Nezamiyeh College and Baghdad, and took an oath at "the sacred dust of Abraham, peace be upon him" (in Hebron) never to return to formal scholastic dialectic. The examples we have quoted – regardless of being factual or fictitious – are much less dramatic than Ghazali's experience, but they help to throw light on the fact that Sa'di quietly left the school and carried on as poet, lover and, eventually, savant.[17]

SA'DI'S DEBATES?

In a story in *Bustan* he names himself as being the narrator (although it may still be fictitious) and is very uncomplimentary about a formal debating society which he claims he had anonymously attended. In chapter four of that book, "On Humility," he tells how a scholar in tattered clothes entered the judge's court and sat in the row of scholars and jurists. The judge gave him a look of disapproval and the official announcer told him "to rise": "Your station is not high, do you not realize [?]/Hesitate not, either leave or rise." He feels humiliated but stays.

A formal debate then begins among the jurists led by the judge. There is much conflict and argumentation but no resolution of the issue is in sight. Then the ragged scholar intervenes. Telling them that instead of "inflating their jugular veins" they should present rational arguments, he solves the problem and when they want to honour him he leaves the court. They then look everywhere for him, and they are told: "A person with breath so sweet/We know only of Sa'di in this town." Not much humility in this last verse, but when he turns down their honours he tells them that if he gives in to temptation he will become vain like them. The story, in its detail at least, is very likely fictitious, but it once again reflects Sa'di's poor view of formal scholastic settings.[18]

There is a certainly fictitious story about a debate in an *informal* setting which tells us much about Sa'di's attitude to life. One of the longest stories of *Golestan,* it is told in the chapter on the effects of education. The narrator meets "one looking like dervishes but lacking their characteristics" in a gathering. The Dervish is engaged in attacking the rich, saying that "the dervish's hands are tied with lack of power and the rich man's legs are broken because of lack of caring for others." The narrator "found these words unpalatable" especially as he himself had been "nurtured by the great." He then launched an eloquent defence of the fortunate, arguing that they were blessed both in this world and the next.

Their blessing in this world is not only due to their good standard of living but especially as they are able to help the poor, support the retired and the recluse, entertain visitors, accommodate strangers visiting their town, give feasts in religious festivals, free slaves, and do other good works. Besides, the rich wear clean clothes, eat well and are not prone to anxiety about their livelihood, all of which affords them the time, the peace of mind and the cleanliness to devote themselves to worship. Hence they are ensured a good placement in the next world as well as this. Poverty, he goes on to argue, is not consistent with peace of mind. There is a religious tradition that says "Poverty brings shame in both worlds."

The Dervish interjected at this point, saying "Have you not heard that the Prophet, peace be upon him, said 'I take honour in poverty'":

> I said 'Silence, since the reference of the lord, peace be upon him, is to the poverty of those who belong to the realm of contentment and are ready to receive what befalls them, not those who wear Sufi attire and sell their allowance grant ... God Great and Almighty describes those who will enjoy Heaven in the indisputable verses of the Qor'an as "the ones who [in this world] enjoy definite provisions." Hence you will know that he whose mind is occupied with the provision of his livelihood lacks the grace of serenity.'

The Dervish exploded, the narrator says, and launched an unmitigated attack on the rich, describing them as proud, arrogant, selfish and conceited, who regarded the *ulama* as beggars, and the poor as worthless; and just "because of the wealth that they possess and the status which they presume to have" they think that they are better than everyone else, and do not acknowledge the existence of anybody besides themselves. The debate continues until the narrator introduces the question of ability (or lack thereof) of the two social categories to enjoy sexual gratification. He argues that as the rich can marry – if they want to, even more than once – their sexual desires are satisfied and they are not likely to slip into sinful behaviour. The same cannot be said for dervishes who may be tempted to resort to sin, since eating and copulation are twin desires such that when one is satisfied the other rises.

> I heard that they arrested a dervish together with a youth on a charge of criminal behaviour. Apart from the shame that the dervish endured there was the threat of being stoned to death. He said 'O' Muslims, I cannot afford to marry, and I am not able to wait, what can I do [?], "There is no celibacy in Islam."'

The debate continues:

> In the end I put him down and he was left with no argument. He lashed his tongue and raised his hand. And it is the habit of the ignorant that when they are void of reasoning they resort to hostile behaviour ... He swore at me and I cursed him. He tore off my collar and I grabbed his chin...

They took their dispute to the judge's court and "consented to the rule of justice."The judge told the narrator:

> You who admired the rich and admonished the poor, know that where there is flower there is thorn, wine results in hangover, and treasures are guarded by serpents; and where there is large pearl there is man-eating shark ... Do you not observe in the garden that there is both fragrant willow and dry wood? Likewise, among the rich are both grateful and ungrateful, and among the poor, both patient and impatient.

The judge then turned to the Dervish and told him the same thing, but in reverse, except that his admonition of the anti-social and ungrateful among the rich was longer and more emphatic. [19]

It is clear that Sa'di's own view of the matter concurs with that of the judge, not just from the text of this story, but also from what we learn about his views through the whole of his works: a fair, generous, even-tempered and optimistic outlook on life and society. In this example he shows that he judges people not by their class or category but by their personal traits and behaviour. In chapter eight of *Golestan*, "On Rules of Conduct," he goes so far as risking the charge of lack of faith when he implies that the claims of Jews and Muslims to truth are relative:

> A Jew and a Muslim were arguing
> Such that their argument made me laugh
> Said the Muslim in anger 'O' God
> If my deed is not true then may I die a Jew'
> The Jew said 'I swear by the Pentateuch
> That if I lie I am a Muslim like you'
> If knowledge disappears from the face of the earth
> Still no-one will suspect that he does not know
> [*Kolliyat*, p. 177.]

Sa'di was a poet, a lover, a man of the world, as well as one who believed in personal propriety and social justice. He was a man of tolerance, moderation, great wit, and good sense, qualities which, added to his outstanding artistic talent, made him better known and more popular in his own time than any other poet. In his works he mentions or alludes to the extent and spread of his popularity in the vast Persian-speaking lands of the time. There is also independent evidence for this. For example, a contemporary letter written in Anatolia (discovered by Mohammad Qazvini) opens with a short stanza by Sa'di, an indication that the stanza in particular, and so his work in general, was famous in that part of the world.

Together with Ferdowsi, Rumi and Hafiz, his fame has been widespread in the Persian cultural region, and his works have been recited and appreciated even by illiterate Persian speakers through the ages. His fame is unique, however, in the fact that he is the only Persian poet about whom the common folk have made up anecdotes and legends, even about his legendary daughter who is supposed to have inherited some of the wit of her great father.

SA'DI AND THE COURTS

For more than fifty years of Sa'di's life, Sa'd ibn Zangi and his son Abubakr ruled Fars. Abubakr's son Sa'd was a patron of Sa'di after the poet's return to Shiraz at the age of fifty. For thirty years of this time Sa'di was travelling in foreign lands and by the time he was sixty the government of Fars had effectively passed to direct rule by the Ilkhanid Mongols. Yet both because of his pen-name and the fact that the Zangis are mentioned and praised and advised in his works, his name is more widely connected to the Zangis than is justified by the length of time over which he was associated with them. As previously noted, Sa'di presented *Golestan* to the young Sa'd. His praise of these rulers is mixed with advice and admonitions, and this is generally the pattern in the case of the relatively few other rulers and important men whom he praised and advised. Both Abubakr and Sa'd died in 1260 and though their dynasty somehow survived till the 1280s power in Fars effectively passed on to the Ilkhan Mongol emperors and the governors they sent to rule the province.

Modern Iranian intellectuals in the twentieth century, influenced by western bourgeois ethics, were often very critical of classical Persian court poets. Two points may be made briefly on this subject. First, until relatively recently most artists, in many cultures, were dependent on the patronage of the great and good so that they could spend their time on their artistic creations. This includes the majority of European painters and musicians up to the nineteenth century. Furthermore, Renaissance paintings, much like classical Persian eulogies for God and man, idealized their subjects such that in religious paintings haloes were drawn around the heads of the sacred images. Even beyond that, many portrait paintings up to the nineteenth century (including those of Napoleon and his generals) tend to idealize their subjects. Putting aside a few exceptions, therefore, these creative artists, be they Persian or European, were neither beggars nor guilty of grotesque exaggerations relative to their time and circumstances. The application of contemporary values to vastly different social and cultural circumstances involves little but idle anachronism.

The second point is that not all classical Persian poets may be described as court poets, and Sa'di should be considered one of this minority, despite the fact that he did go to the court and did write occasional eulogies. The court poets *par excellence* were like those who functioned as such under the great Ghaznavids – Onsori, Farrokhi, Manuchehri, for example – whose main function as poets was to praise their patrons and describe their wars, festivities and such like in their poetry. There is much genuine feeling and emotion even in the court poetry of these poets, quite apart from their excellent command over poetical forms and their passionate descriptions of love and nature, which normally preceded their eulogies. Occasionally, one finds eulogies by them that are void of feelings, such as some of those by Anvari. There were also real and practising mystic poets totally unconnected with courts and patrons – such as Attar and Rumi – but they either had means of their own or were supported by their devotees.

Despite his connection with the courts, Sa'di was not a court poet for two principal reasons. First, the number of his poems addressed to great men (and two women, Turkan Khatun and her daughter Abesh Khatun of the Solghorids) is negligible compared to the rest of his works. Secondly, even his praises are often mixed with advice and admonition to the powerful to be just and generous. For example, in

Bustan where he is indirectly admonishing the then ruler Abubakr, he
realizes that he has been too outspoken, but then he adds that that is
how it should be, for someone who is free from greed and who does
not take bribes should speak the truth:

> Boldly have you come to speak O' Sa'di
> Do make a conquest now that you hold the sword
> Say what you know, since the truth is best told:
> You neither take bribe nor give blandishments
> Give up wisdom if you surrender to greed
> You can speak out when freed from greed

Amir Angiyanu was the powerful Mongol governor of Fars between
1268 and 1271 or 1272. His brief rule was typical of that of a strong
man after a period of chaos: he would restore stability and rule with
an iron fist. A number of eminent citizens complained to the Mongol
emperor about Angiyanu's methods, which led to his recall to the
imperial capital. Sa'di wrote three *qasideh*s addressed to this Amir.
These are normally cited in his collected works as eulogies but in fact
they are admonitions and, in some verses, dire warnings. He begins
the longest and best known by saying that the world never remains
constant and therefore intelligent people do not become strongly
attached to it. The reason why legends such as those of Rostam and
Esfandiyar are told, is for rulers to learn that there have been many
before them, to teach them a lesson about the transience of life. He
then issues a dire warning:

> You who were once a foetus
> Next, a suckling babe
> Then grew and matured
> Like a tall tree, a cypress
> Till you became famous
> A knight in the arts of war and chase.
> The past remained not at the same phase
> Nor will the present remain the same
> Sooner or later this dear person
> Will turn into earth, then into dust…
> Better to leave a good name
> Than a palace of gold behind…

> They write eulogies for rulers
> I give you advice, dervish-like…
> [*Kolliyat*, pp. 724–725.]

In another *qasideh* addressed to Angiyanu he writes on much the same lines, and issues similar warnings:

> There is much earth stepped on unawares
> That if you dig you will find hand and wrist…
> They turn the dust of humans into bricks
> Yet, forewarned, their hearts tremble not

He goes so far that he feels he must give a word of reassurance that only he, Sa'di, could dare to speak so directly and vehemently:

> Not all could speak the truth so bold
> Words are the realm, Sa'di is the lord
> [*Kolliyat*, pp. 732–733.]

And finally in the last of the three Angiyanu *qasideh*s:

> Life is not worth your breaking a heart
> Do no wrong, as would no man who is smart…
> Of the masses of wealth and treasure
> They took to their grave not one measure…
> Death is close to you, be it as it may
> You take another step towards it every day
> [*Kolliyat* pp. 755–757.]

Not all of Sa'di's eulogies and addresses to the mighty are so full of warnings and admonitions, but virtually all of them contain an element of it. However, the number of such poems among Sa'di's works is very small. It is clear that Sa'di was neither a sycophant nor a court poet.[20]

WORKS

Sa'di's works are made up principally of the two books *Bustan* and *Golestan*, the four books of *ghazal*, his Persian and Arabic *qasideh*s, and his quatrains and short pieces, and some other works in prose and poetry. His first two books are especially well known, both in Iran and elsewhere, and this has led to an underestimation and lack of study of his other works, particularly his *ghazals*, which are both numerous and, among the classics, virtually unmatched as expressions of human (as distinct from mystic) love.

Bustan

This book was finished in 1257 (655) when the poet was fifty or more years old and had returned from a thirty-year odyssey in much of the Islamic lands. It is in verse in the *mathnavi* form. *Mathnavi* is a poem of any length in short meters consisting of couplets which rhyme in the form of AA, BB, CC, and so on. For example, here are verses from chapter four, "On Humility":

> Someone was holding a fiddle, drunk
> At night he broke it on the head of a monk
> Next day the patient good parson
> Took some money to the cruel person
> Said last night you were drunk and excusable
> Of me the head broke and of you the fiddle
> My wound has healed and fear lifted
> Only with money will yours be shifted
> [*Kollyat*, p. 318.]

It should be noted that there are of course no "monks" and "parsons" as such in Islam, and these terms have been used here for the sake of rhyme, while maintaining the meaning of the poem.

Mathnavi is the most popular form of narrative poetry, and was used to write epic, romance, mystical and didactive poetry. Its meters are varied but usually short. Both *Bustan* and Ferdowsi's *Shahnameh* are in the *mathnavi* form, and both are in the same meter. The mystical narratives of Sana'i, Attar and Rumi, and the narrative romances of Gorgani and Nezami are also in this form, but their meters are often different among themselves, and, except for one book of Nezami, different from *Bustan* and *Shahnameh*. Short meters and the use of various rhymes relative to *qasideh* and *ghazal* make *mathnavi* the ideal classical form for writing long and continuous poems in which a story, or series of stories, is usually told.

There grew an attitude among modernist Iranian intellectuals to dismiss such works as *Shahnameh*, *Bustan* and Rumi's *Mathnavi* as sheer versification, not deserving to be described as poetry, although they would not likewise regard narrative poetry by writers such as Shakespeare, Racine, Corneille or Goethe as mere versification. However, *Bustan's* poetical forms are well developed. Apart from the meter and rhyme being almost perfect throughout, there is a wealth of figures of speech – or "literary devices" as they are called by the modern formalists – which afford the narrative its poetical quality. A remarkable skill of Sa'di over and above any other classical Persian poets and writers is the amazing brevity with which he expresses himself in verse as well as prose. Often, poetical accounts and descriptions are put forth with much clarity and eloquence in considerably fewer words than it would take to present them in other forms. It is described as the art of "the easy and impossible" (*sahl o momtane'*) in classical Persian criticism.

Bustan has been described as didactive, moralistic and mystical. This itself is evidence that it does not easily fall into any of those categories even though it does deal with morals, rules of conduct and mystical concepts and experiences. It is, from this point of view, a unique volume in the whole canon of Persian literature. It has been imitated and copied by other authors such as Fath'ali Khan Saba in his *Nasihatnameh*, but there is no other original work which is quite comparable to it. Sana'i's *Haqiat al-Haqiqa* (Garden of Truth) – written before *Bustan* in the twelfth century – is not quite the same kind of book as is sometimes believed; it is a crypto-mystical volume which anticipates some of Attar's and, to a lesser degree, Rumi's works. Comparisons – as suggested by some western scholars – with such "mirrors for princes" as Keikavus ibn Eskandar's *Qabusnameh* and Nezam al-Molk's *Siyasatnameh* (both of them twelfth-century prose works) are even more far-fetched. And if there is some kind of correspondence between *Bustan* and Ghazali's *Nasihat al-Moluk* (written at the turn of the twelfth century) it should be confined only to the first chapter of the former book. It is, unlike *Golestan*, also a theoreti-

cal book dealing with ideals, even though it discusses issues arising
from real human life and conduct. Hence the oft-repeated view that
while it is to some extent true of *Golestan* that Sa'di's works display
"practical wisdom," it does not apply to *Bustan*.

There are just a few pages (in chapter five) in which the poet
attempts but does not succeed to present reasonable epic poetry. It
begins convincingly enough when he says that someone had said he
was an excellent poet but only as regarded moral subjects, not the
epic, "which has been perfected by others" (presumably meaning
Ferdowsi). He then responds in suitably epic terms by saying:

> He knows not that we do not wish to challenge
> Else the scope of our words is wide to arrange
> I can unleash the dagger of the tongue
> And a torrent of words my pen will prong
> Let us take up the challenge in this field
> And make a pillow of the enemy's head
> [*Kolliyat*, p. 322.]

In spite of this rather promising start there follow two stories, poor
in content and even weak in form, both uncharacteristic of Sa'di's
work. It is clear from these two stories and others which follow
them that, despite his conditioned response to take up the challenge, Sa'di simply does not have his heart in writing epics and in
epic virtues. This he reveals most eloquently and unambiguously in
the opening verses of chapter seven "On the Realm of Edification,"
where he says:

> The subject is good sense and habit
> Not horse, polo, ball and battlefield
> You live with your enemy, your carnal self
> Why should you fight the stranger then?
> Those who deny their carnal self the forbidden
> Surpass Rostam and Sam in chivalry and honour[21]
> [*Kolliyat*, p. 342.]

Apart from the introductory pieces, the book is in ten chapters, each
containing a number of tales, anecdotes or stories. It begins with an
introduction that, as noted, contains its dedication to the people of

Shiraz. It also contains a list of the ten chapters in verse. Chapter one is "On Justice, Sound Government and Good Judgement"; chapter two, "On Beneficence"; chapter three, "On Love, Intoxication and Ecstasy"; chapter four, "On Humility"; chapter five, "On Resignation"; chapter six, "On Contentment"; chapter seven, "On the Realm of Edification"; chapter eight, "On Gratitude for Well-being"; chapter nine, "On Repentance and the Right Course"; chapter ten, "On Personal Communion and Conclusion of the Book."

Golestan

This book is the best known and most popular of Sa'di's works. This is the one book by Sa'di which, if any book can, might be described as a source of "practical wisdom," although its style and scope goes well beyond that. It is principally in prose and consists of an introduction and eight chapters. Chapter one is "On the Manners of Rulers"; chapter two, "On the Morals of Dervishes"; chapter three, "On the Virtues of Contentment"; chapter four, "On the Advantages of Silence"; chapter five, "On Love and Youth"; chapter six, "On Weakness and Old Age"; chapter seven, "On the Effects of Education"; chapter eight, "On Rules of Conduct." These chapters, like those of *Bustan*, which was presented in public the year before, consist of stories, tales and anecdotes, sometimes told in the first person singular.

Although they are in prose, they are normally adorned with verses which often heighten in shorthand and epigrammatic form what has just been expressed in prose. On a few occasions the whole of the tale consists of a short poem, not longer than twelve couplets but usually shorter than that. For example, the following poem from chapter two combines brevity, depth and beauty all at once:

Someone told he who had lost his son [Jacob]
O' enlightened wise old don
You sensed the scent of his [Joseph's] garment from Egypt
Why did you not see him in the well of Canaan?
Our mind is just like lightning, he said
Sometimes it shines sometimes it is dead

> Sometimes we sit on a pedestal high
> Sometimes we fail to see our foot and thigh
> If in ecstasy the dervish remained
> He would rise beyond the two worlds
> [*Kolliyat*, p. 75.]

The prose style or genre is *mosajja'*, a most ornate form of prose with occasional meters of varying short lengths and occasional rhymes or semi-rhymes. Here are a few examples from A. J. Arberry's translation of the first two chapters of the book, *Kings and Beggars*:

> Better a Wiseman short of bulk, than a huge and witless hulk.

> The sheep is neat and clean; the elephant a mass obscene.

> O king, in splendour we are less than you in the world here present, yet in our life more pleasant; at death we are your equal and better at the Resurrection Sequel.

And here are some other examples rendered by this author:

> He who washes his hands of life speaks whatever he has in heart.

> He who hurts God Almighty to please one created by him, God will appoint the same person to get rid of him.

> To eat one's own bread sitting, better than be in high service standing.

This prose style is easily prone to two kinds of weaknesses: first, becoming too artificial in its embellishments; second, the form overshadowing the substance. Perhaps for these very reasons it has been seldom used, and no-one that has used it has been as completely successful as Sa'di in avoiding such weaknesses, so that, in his hands, a prose as ornate as that nevertheless is both fluent and comprehensible. The quality of brevity combined with fluency and elegance that is found in *Bustan* as a poem — the art of "easy and impossible" noted above — is likewise found in *Golestan* as a book of prose. Sa'di is virtually unique in his near-perfect application of this art both in poetry and prose. Iraj Mirza, the early-twentieth-century poet, approaches it in his work.

Golestan raises virtually every major issue faced by humankind through stories, anecdotes and maxims which are at once enlightening, witty and entertaining. It contains much – subtle as opposed to coarse – verbal and dramatic satire, an art in which Sa'di excels, and of which he is one of the earliest Persian masters. It indicates the ways to good, clean living in a world which, considerably more so than in *Bustan*, is shown to be imperfect. Yet the impression gained from both these books is that their author has a positive if not optimistic outlook, finds life well worth living, and believes that the world could be a much better place if its human inhabitants had a little more regard and compassion for one another. The following stanza from *Golestan* is universally famous:

> Children of Adam belong to one another
> Who, in creation, are of the same basic matter
> When one member is hurt by an act of fate
> Other members cannot remain free of hurt
> You who are mindless of others' pain
> Do not deserve to be called human
> [*Kolliyat*, p. 47.]

The introduction to *Golestan* is a literary gem in its own right. In it is an account of how the book came into being, with remarkable implications that so far have gone unnoticed. He says with his characteristic brevity and economy that one night he was reflecting on his life and feeling sad about the time he had "wasted." He then says in verse that he had put fifty or more years behind him and yet he felt that he was completely "empty handed":

> You who are past fifty and are still unawares
> Perhaps you will learn in the remaining few days...
> Life is like snow melting by the mid-summer sun
> Just a little of it remains yet the man is still vain
> You who have gone to the bazaar with empty hands
> I fear you will not return with a basket of goods

He says he was so depressed that torrents of tears were falling down his cheeks, "like diamonds making holes in my chest." He decided to turn into a recluse and not "speak nonsense" any more, until a close friend of his arrived. At first, no matter how much he tried the friend drew no response from the poet. A member of the household told him of Sa'di's decision to remain aloof and quiet, but the friend did not give up and eventually convinced him to go out in the country with him. It was the twenty-first day of April (1258) he says precisely, and the weather and nature were breathtakingly beautiful:

> Twenty-first of April, of the solar calendar
> The nightingale singing on tree branches
> Pearls of water spread on the red rose
> Just like sweat on the beloved's angry face

They spent the night in the country. Next day when they set out to return, his friend gathered a bunch of flowers to take back to town. Sa'di told him that flowers are perishable but he could compose a rose garden (*golestan*) that would remain permanently immune from the passage of time; and added in verse:

> What of a bunch of flowers, if you pardon?
> Take a leaf instead from my Rose Garden
> Flowers will remain only for a few days
> This Rose Garden will be fresh always

The friend begged him to fulfil his promise. He began to write that very day and finished the book by the end of the summer.[22]

What can we make of this account? It is not impossible that the whole thing is fiction, but this is unlikely since he is describing precisely how the work came to be written and there is no reason why he should make up such a story. He needed no excuse for writing a book which in his own estimation would remain for ever, and which, when completed, he presented to the heir apparent of the realm just as he had presented *Bustan* to his fellow citizens the year before. It is more likely that he was genuinely depressed, perhaps suffering from a form of "post-natal depression" after the publication of *Bustan*, which sometimes happens when a work of art is completed and "abandons" its author. Then a friend or friends came to his aid and boosted his morale so that he began to recover after a visit to the country. He then decided to fill the vacuum in his spirit by writing the new book and was soon elated to a point that enabled him to finish the book in the short period of only five to six months. It is reminiscent of so many great works of art having come into being after their authors had gone through a period of depression. If his account is not pure fiction then this analysis must be broadly true, especially as it also explains the surprisingly short length of time which it took to complete the book.[23]

The ghazals

Ghazal is the poetry of love-songs and lyrics for the beloved in both human and mystical love. It is a mono-rhyme poem of between five and fifteen couplets which come in various meters and rhymes in the form of AA, BA, CA, and so on. Sa'di is a master of *ghazal* and together with Hafiz and Rumi they make up the three greatest *ghazal* writers of Persian poetry. His style is completely original and made an impact on the writings of Hafiz, although the latter's *ghazals* are also unique and original. We shall discuss Sa'di's *ghazals* in chapter 3.

The qasidehs

Qasideh is a long poem, usually more than sixteen couplets and often much longer. It, too, is a mono-rhyme poem written in virtually any meter in the Persian prosody, and its rhyming scheme is the same as *ghazal*. It is the most formal genre of classical Persian poetry and was fully developed in the eleventh and twelfth centuries in the hands of such masters as Farrokhi, Manuchehri, Anvari and Khaqani. It is a poem of formal and solemn subjects such as eulogy, elegy, stylized nature description and, less often, moral and intellectual reflection. By Sa'di's time the heyday of *qasideh* had passed and *ghazal* and *mathnavi* had replaced it as the principal forms of poetry, a fact which also represents the shift in the content and substance of poetry to lyricism, romances and ethical and mystical tales and stories.

Sa'di is perhaps the last great *qasideh* writer until the nineteenth century when there was a movement for the restoration of the traditions and styles of the old masters (from the tenth to the sixteenth century). His *qasideh*s are impeccable in form but are limited in number and lack the Olympian solemnity of those of the previous masters. Their subject is eulogy, elegy, lament, description of nature, reflection and admonition.

Other works

Sa'di has a fairly considerable number of quatrains, short stanzas, short *mathnavi*s and single couplets. He also has a couple of *tarji'band*s, long poems consisting of a number of stanzas connected by a refraining couplet. There are also a number of *qasideh*s in Arabic, a few written in a mixture of Persian and Arabic, and one *mathnavi* which is in Persian and Arabic as well as the Shirazi dialect of his time. There are also six essays in his collected works, a couple of which might have been added by others although it is more likely that they too are by his own pen.

We shall not pursue the *qasideh*s and the other works in this book, except on a few occasions.

3

SONGS OF LOVE AND ODES TO BEAUTY

No classical Persian poet was a greater and more passionate lover than Sa'di. One may even make the higher claim that he was the greatest lover, certainly the greatest lyricist of human love, in classical Persian poetry. Yet the impact of *Bustan* and *Golestan* has been so great that they have overshadowed his work as a poet of love songs. Not only have they been seldom translated into western languages compared with those two books, especially *Golestan*, but even in Iran Sa'di's *ghazals* have never been appreciated as much as they deserve, except in traditional Persian singing. Along with Hafiz and Rumi, as before, Sa'di, is one of the three greatest Persian *ghazal* writers of all time.

Sa'di is the champion of human love, the love of the flesh; Rumi the champion of mystical love, of the Sufi longing for the return to and reunion with the origins of all existence. Hafiz integrates the two such that often in the same piece they are both expressed with equal passion, or it is the case that the expression of one type of love implies the existence of the other, there being two layers of meaning in the same verse. Many classical critics and scholars, both Persian and western, have tended to interpret Sa'di's love poetry as mystical.

For example, the late British scholar Reynold Nicholson expressed this view while adding, not surprisingly, that while Sa'di's lyricism is great his mysticism is shallow.[24] Iranian scholar and poet Rashid Yasemi has also described the whole of Sa'di's *ghazals* as mystical and esoteric, but unlike Nicholson he finds them profound and convincing.[25]

Such views seem to be based on the traditional misconception that virtually all lyrical Persian poetry has a hidden mystical meaning. Furthermore, nineteenth- and early twentieth-century Iranian scholars tended to believe that the great Persian classics were all chaste, sexless and entirely ascetic, and that any worldly interest and passion was beneath their exalted position. Many western scholars, though perhaps they did not go as far as that, generally followed the views of Persian scholars over the basic mystical quality of much of the lyricism of the great classics.

This view flies in the face of the facts certainly in the case of Sa'di, the bulk of whose *ghazals* are patently about the love of the flesh, and that of both sexes, as we shall see. Of his more than seven hundred *ghazals*, about ten percent fall into the mystical-cum-ethical category. The rest are based on his rich and enviable love experience. But this does not mean that every piece is autobiographical, reflecting a concrete experience of union or separation with a lover, any more than the mystical *ghazals* may be assumed to be immediate responses to a mystical experience.

Love may be an abstract mood as well as a concrete experience. What Sa'di's *ghazals* on human love reflect is more realistically his general experience of human love, both physical and mental, rather than definite biographical details of such experience, although some of them may well have been such. Poetry, either in part or as a whole, often contains more than one layer of meaning, which can be discovered or approximated only by a close study of its tropes, symbolism, metaphors, imagery and the like. There is no scope in this study for conducting such analyses for Sa'di's individual *ghazals*. What follows is a general discussion of his love songs taken as a whole.

THE EVOLUTION OF POETRY

By Sa'di's time in the thirteenth century all forms of Persian poetry (including *qasideh, ghazal, mathnavi,* and quatrains) had been developed, all the variety of figures of speech (such as metaphor, imagery, simile, allusion and pun) had been applied, and all subjects (including panegyrics, romances, epics and mysticism) had been tried. Nevertheless, there had been a continuous evolution, such that all these forms, techniques and subjects had undergone significant changes. Rumi's mystical poetry in the thirteenth century was not quite the same in form or content as Sana'i's and Attar's in the twelfth. That is also true of other forms and subjects, but especially of *ghazal* and love poetry. Sa'di perfected the form of *ghazal*, such that until this day his style has not been bettered. Over time, from the tenth to the thirteenth century, the content of the *ghazal* has changed, since love itself evolves in concept and implications.

In the amorous lyricism of the eleventh-century poets, for example, the beloved appears to be equal if not frequently subordinate to the lover and poet. Farrokhi opens a lyrical piece by announcing "I made up with my beloved after a long war." He says in another that the beloved bowed to him, whereas in later periods the poet-and-lover is definitely subordinate to the beloved in their relationship even if his social station is above her or him. Sa'di opens a *ghazal* by saying "Who am I the lowly person to desire your hand?" and Hafiz (in the fourteenth century) says in a verse "When the beloved ignores you, try to offer her more."

The same difference may be found even in the romances that are stories of legendary rather than personal love. For example, both Ferdowsi (tenth to eleventh century) and Nezami (twelfth century) have told the story of the love of Khosraw and Shirin. Yet Nezami's account is far more lofty and colourful than Ferdowsi's, which looks more like a historical narrative. Even in Nezami's account, the lovers are still equal, and their love still not as romantic as that of Farhad for Shirin, who is in fact much lower in station than his beloved.

One important cause of this development must be due to the growth of Sufism in the twelfth and, especially, the thirteenth centuries, since mystic love is by definition that of a seeker abjectly aspiring to union with the exalted and virtually unreachable beloved. In other words, the language and passion of mystic poetry is likely to have influenced the language of love. Some have gone further and claimed that the expression of human love itself is everywhere a worldly form of expressing desire for the mystical beloved, or that the beloved in what looks like human love simply acts as a symbol for the mystic object of loving. This seems unlikely, and is mere speculation.

SA'DI, HAFIZ, RUMI

Sa'di's enthusiasm and his passion for the love of fellow human beings flows through his love songs, although not as much as the ecstatic outbursts that are sometimes observed in Rumi's *ghazals*, normally addressed to Shams in the image of the mystical beloved. As noted, the *gahzals* of Sa'di, Rumi and Hafiz are somewhat different from each other, and each is unique in its own style, although many poets have been influenced by them. In their hands, Persian *ghazal* reaches its summit. Rumi's works are often passionate in tone and musical in meter, confirming reports that many of them were written down by disciples while the poet uttered the words as he was whirling round a column. Sa'di's are almost perfect in form and technique – being the first group of *ghazals* written at this high level – and are about joys of love, ecstasy of being in union with the beloved, and sadness of separation. The use and application of figures of speech or literary devices are so masterly that the poems contain words and meaning at their loftiest and most artistic level. However, Sa'di's *ghazals* are, while technically of such high quality, also sweet in form and uncomplicated in content, such that they are not difficult to read and enjoy.

The *ghazal* of Hafiz is likewise impeccable in form but normally contains more than one theme, so that both mystic and human love as well as a eulogy for an important person – but especially his beloved Shah Shoja'– may be found in the same single piece. It usually combines the mystic and human love so well that it would not be easy to tell one from the other. Finally, in the *ghazal* of Hafiz the use of rather complicated, though highly competent, metaphor and imagery – which was to be further extended by the best of the poets of the "Indian Style" – gives it an ambiguous, sometimes even enigmatic, character. This accounts for much of the fascination of readers for his poetry, including its regular use by them in a fortune-telling text.

There follow parts of three *ghazals* by Sa'di, Rumi and Hafiz as brief examples for a comparison of their love poetry. This will, inevitably, be partial and incomplete, and we shall quote other examples of Sa'di's *ghazals* later in this chapter.

Sa'di

Stop being drunk, all my life I will not
For I was not born when you entered my sight
Unlike the sun you do not come and go
Others come and go, you permanently glow
What pain I endured of our separation
Your face shone and ended the damnation...
Go away learned doctor, leave us to the Almighty
Us, loving and drunkenness, you, prayer and piety
[*Kolliyat*, p. 606.]

Hafiz

Your beauty shone at the creation's dawn
Love appeared, on fire the entire world thrown
Reason tried to use that fire to make a light
The lightening of disdain set the world alight
The stranger tried to come to the sight of mystery
The hidden hand stretched and put him to misery ...
My celestial soul longed for the dimple of your chin
The curls of your hair it put its hand in
[Divan-e Hafiz]

Rumi

I was dead I came alive I was tears I became smile
The kingdom of love came and I became eternally alive
I have the eye of lion I have the soul of the brave
The courage of lion, I am Venus shining bright

You do not belong here, said he, you are not insane
I went away, went mad and put myself in chain
You are not drunk, said he, not of this cut
I went and got drunk, drowned myself in delight...
[Divan-e Shams]

The purpose, content and substance of Sa'di's ethical-cum-mystical *ghazals* is a mixture of mystical and ethical reflections, guidance and admonition, but they certainly do not compare with those of the leading Sufi *ghazal* writers in depth, enthusiasm and passion. They show his knowledge of, respect for and sympathy with genuine mystical thoughts and feelings, but they also show that he is not personally immersed in mystical experience. They are impeccable in form as is the rest of his poetry, and competent and effective in their meaning, but they do not move the enthusiastic reader to great heights of ecstasy and passion, as does some of his poetry for those who are moved by the passion of human loving. The following examples may be compared with some Sufi *ghazals*, including one by Rumi that we have quoted above.

The following *ghazal* on the potential of humanity to rise up above the status of angels contains general mystical lessons and admonitions, but (especially in the Persian original) in a highly elevated language: "How as a human became you captive to demons?/Not even angels can rise up to man's potential."

The place of humanity

The human body is ennobled by the human soul
You will not be human just wearing a nice shawl
If eye, mouth, ear and nose, define a human being
What is the difference between man and a picture on the wall?
Eating, sleeping, anger, passion are darkness and ignorance
Animals have no knowledge of the world of humanity at all
Try to be a human being in reality, otherwise a parrot
May effect the human beings' language, speech and call
How as a human became you captive to a demon?
Not even angels can rise up to man's potential
If the cannibalism in your nature dies and disappears

You will be always alive through the human soul
Man may reach a point of seeing no one but God
Look how may man's place be exalted and tall
Birds fly, free yourself from the fetters of passion
To see how human beings can fly like them all
[*Kolliyat*, pp. 789–790.]

This next *ghazal* on the kingdom of beggars is more specific, though still quite familiar, pointing out the morals, attitude and behaviour which will result in mystical fulfilment and liberation. It also shows more directly the ethical and religious context within which the mystic path must travel: "On the Day of Judgement he will be clothed/Who in this world is naked, lacks adornment."

The kingdom of beggars

There is no life as royal as that of beggars
No kingdom is more stable than contentment
If anyone has real dignity it is he
Who lacks dignity in anyone's assessment
Everyone has a character, a colour, a creed
Give them all up, that is the best arrangement
On the Day of Judgement he will be clothed
Who in this world is naked, lacks adornment
Who is he who enjoys any knowledge at all?
It is he who knows no one, who is self-sufficient
The stone and the vegetation which are of some use
Are better than the man who affords no-one fulfilment
You are unaware of your luck, O' dervish
Rejoice that you do not have; that is your interest
He is not a lover who complains of the beloved
Blood shed by the beloved knows no compensation
Good manners are these which are taught by Sa'di
If you listen you will have no better education
[*Kolliyat*, p. 789.]

The following *ghazal* may be put in either category, human and mystical love, both elements being closely interwoven in it. For that reason, as well as the fact that it contains various themes, it anticipates many that are similar to it that were written by Hafiz decades later: "Those who during Ramadan banned music/Heard the flower breathe and joined the frenzy."

Love in spring

> Trees are in bloom, nightingales are drunk
> The world has turned young, friends in joyful truck
> Full of charm was always our drinking partner
> Now adorned, she is more charming than ever
> Those who during Ramadan banned music
> Heard the flower breathe and joined the frenzy
> Feet have beaten down the lawn delightfully
> By the mystic's and non-mystic's dance joyously
> Two friends will appreciate friendship's fire
> Who parted for a while then got back in desire
> No-one sober leaves the Sufis' court (*khaneqah*)
> To tell the police that Sufis are inebriate
> In our exclusive space there is a floral tree
> More balanced in figure than the cypress tree
> If the whole world becomes my enemy, I swear
> By my beloved that of none of them I'll be aware
> He whom love has killed looks like seafarers
> Who dropped their cargo and survived themselves
> The cypress tree was asked why it bore no fruit
> The free, it replied, are empty in hand and foot
> Many, O' Sa'di, took the road to Rationality
> Because they knew not the path of Insanity
> [*Kolliyat*, p. 606.]

We shall postpone a comprehensive discussion of Sa'di's approach and attitude towards Sufism to the next chapter.

WOMEN AND YOUTHS

Sa'di's lyrics on love of the flesh come in four groups: those which express love for the beloved, those which describe the beloved, those which express the joy of union, and those which reflect the sadness of separation.

The beloved may be either a woman or a youth. Since there is no distinction between the masculine and feminine genders in the Persian language, there being a common third person pronoun for males and females, it is not always readily clear whether it is a "he" or a "she" to whom the poet is referring. But often there are indicators that define the gender of the beloved. In the case of women the clearest indicator is when the poet mentions their veil (*burka, neqab, pardeh, hejab*), but there can be other indicators as well.

In the following couplet, the beloved has been likened to Shirin, Khosraw's beloved Armenian wife:

Certainly you are the contemporary Shirin
I am the slave of the Khosraw of the time
[*Kolliyat*, p. 566.]

Here the lover says that he will only stop watching the beloved if she puts on a veil:

I have no intention to take my eyes off you
Unless you stop the riot by covering your face
[*Kolliyat*, p. 560.]

Here the lover refers to his being caught, exposed, as the beloved's lover:

She took the veil off my love suddenly
The one who is hidden in a veil
[*Kolliyat*, p. 442.]

In the following the lover laments the beloved wearing a veil, even a garment:

It is a pity for that body to be covered
It is injustice for that face to be veiled
[*Kolliyat*, p. 421.]

In this couplet he compares the projection of the beloved's face to a morning breeze:

Do you know why I love the morning breeze?
It feels as if the beloved has taken off her veil
[*Kolliyat*, p. 604.]

In the following couplet the beloved's face is so radiant that if she removed her veil she would shine even in daylight:

A face which if it sheds the veil in daylight
Will be shining like a star in a dark night
[*Kolliyat*, p. 617.]

Here the beloved could hunt and capture people just by taking her veil off:

You need no lasso for hunting people
It is just enough if you drop the veil
[*Kolliyat*, p. 636.]

In the following the beloved should wear a veil or no pious person will remain in the realm:

If with that beauty you do not cover your face
Never again will you see a pious person in Fars
[*Kolliyat*, p. 419.]

Here, the beloved is begged to drop her veil so that the work of God may be admired by all:

Do not for God's sake hide your face from man and woman
Let them see the work of God from left and right
[*Kolliyat*, p. 428.]

This one contains a similar theme:

I wish the veil fell off that site of beauty
So everyone could see the picture gallery
[*Kolliyat*, p. 417.]

And finally, even the veil will not quite hide the beloved's beauty:

The angel-face will not hide from view
Even if she veils herself a hundred times
[*Kolliyat*, p. 604.]

Love and admiration for the youth is not a characteristic of Sa'di's poetry alone, it is found in the entire nexus of classical Persian poetry. Although it involves love for people of the same gender it does not have the personal, social and cultural implications of male homosexuality in the West. Two types of such love may be distinguished. One is the love of Sufis and other mystics for youths – purportedly as symbols of the beauty of God – as well as the expression of love, often in a passionate language, for their pupils, disciples and fellow Sufis of any age. The case of Rumi's love for his mentor Shams is well known. Indeed most of his enormous number of *ghazals* are addressed to Shams and contain expressions of love for him. But he also expresses passionate love for other male persons among his friends and admirers both in his *Mathnavi* and in his *ghazals*. A most passionate and explicit example is the *ghazal* in which he expresses love for his friend and disciple Hesam al-Din Chalabi:

> You do not ask after me, o' Chalabi you tease me
> How much must I suffer, o' Chalabi you tease me
> O' Chalabi you tease me, I wish to overpower you
> Alas your drunken eye, o' Chalabi you tease me
> Elsewhere you have desire, with me you are fire
> Wild and saucy you are, o' Chalabi you tease me
> You deceived me much, left me and ran off
> You shed my blood; o' Chalabi you tease me...
> [Divan-e Shams]

The other type of love for young men is love and admiration for the beauty, freshness, very youth, intelligence and intellect of young male persons with whom the poet and philosopher associated as mentor, teacher, pupil and young companion. Like the first type, it often used a language much like the love for women, but it did not usually involve sexual relations. It corresponds to the classical Greek tradition, not of contemporary western homosexuality, nor of male paedophilia, but of love and admiration for academic pupils which was regarded as a higher love than that for women, and which seldom involved an actual physical relationship. This does not mean that such physical relationships never happened but that the love expressed by the poets and philosophers did not normally involve such experiences. Sa'di says in *Bustan* that some people associate with young men claiming that theirs is a higher love. Whereas, he indicates by metaphor, they are hiding the fact that they use them as substitutes for the female company they would prefer but of which they are deprived: "The plough ox has its head in the straw/because its rope does not reach the sesame seeds."[26]

Once again the gender in the love poems is not explicit because of the absence of gender-specific personal pronouns, but in some cases there are indicators that show the beloved is a young man. One of these is the word *khatt*, literally meaning line, but representing the early growth of hair above the youth's lips that in adulthood will turn into a moustache. It is sometimes used in the form of "green line" (*khatt-e sabz*) and of "grass of the line" (*sabzeh-ye khatt*), alluding to the colour of the early moustache in someone with dark hair. In a verse Sa'di likens the *khatt* to a line drawn by a pen that uses dust instead of ink.

Another frequently used term is *shahed*, meaning "witness" who is present in the company and is witness to esoteric beauty; *shahed-bazi* literally means "playing with *shahed*," i.e. love and affection for youths. Other indicative terms are *nazar* and *nazarbazi*. *Nazar* literally means "look," *nazarbazi*, "looking-play"; *nazarbaz* like *shahed-baz* is one who is or is inclined to be involved with youths. *Sahab-nazar* literally means "the person who looks" and has the same implication as *nazar-baz* and *shahed-baz*. All of them refer exclusively to the love of youths and, as noted, usually imply a loving admiration rather than overt sexual passion, although we saw that this was also a possibility. Among the great classics, these terms are especially found in the love poetry of Sa'di and Hafiz.

Khatt

The following couplet uses the phrase "grass of the line" to refer to the beloved's newly grown *khatt*:

> Sa'di loves the grass of the *khatt*
> Unlike animals that just love the grass
> [*Kolliyat*, p. 418.]

In the following couplet "green line" has been used to praise the beauty of the beloved:

> Sa'di loves a green khatt
> In the vicinity of a red cheek
> [*Kolliyat*, p. 638.]

Khatt also means "script" and "hand-writing," and is used in a pun in some verses, apparently meaning "script" or "hand-writing," but in fact meaning the youth's "line":

> Good hand-writing (*khatt*) is a chapter in your qualities
> Sweetness among your qualities is a letter in a book
> [*Kolliyat*, p. 603.]

Here is another example of the same pun:

> The mystics of Fars bow to your hand-writing (*khatt*)
> Have you been writing a verse by Sa'di?
> [*Kolliyat*, p. 594.]

In the following couplet the ruby lips and green *khatt* of the beloved are likened to the Spring of Immortality:

> How would you describe your green *khatt* and ruby lips?
> I liken them to the side of the Spring of Immortality
> [*Kolliyat*, p. 491.]

In this couplet the beloved has a mole on the right hand side of his mouth; bear in mind that Persian script is written from right to left:

> Your perfumed *khatt* and your mole look as if
> The pen of dust was moving and it dripped a drop
> [*Kolliyat*, p. 632.]

Shahed, nazar, nazar-bazi *and* sahab-nazar

In the following couplet the poet takes pride in his own *shahed-bazi*, his admiration and love for good-looking and intelligent youths:

Everywhere Sa'di is known for *shahed-bazi*
This in our creed is not a fault but an achievement
[*Kolliyat*, p. 458.]

Here he advises himself to be both a recluse and a *shahed-baz*:

Be a recluse and a *shahedbaz*, o' Sa'di
He is a *shahed* who visits the recluse
[*Kolliyat*, p. 476.]

In the following couplet "Turk" is used to mean fair and light-skinned,
and Frankish to mean European:

There is no *shahed* as merry as my beloved Turk
Frankish loop is not as good as his curly hair
[*Kolliyat*, p. 458.]

The following contains an excellent imagery:

A *shahed* with a candle is pure riot
Being also sleepy and drunk
[*Kolliyat*, p. 421.]

In this couplet even the *mohtaseb*, the chief officer enforcing religious
law, is mentioned in connection with admirers of youths:

Mohtaseb is pursuing the libertine
Mindless of the *shahed-baz* Sufis
[*Kolliyat*, p. 525.]

In the following the lover shows concern about potential competition:

Tonight that the mystics' feast
Is lighted by the candle of your face
Be quiet so the *shahaed-baz* libertines
Do not get to hear about it
[*Kolliyat*, p. 415.]

The following contains both the related terms *nazar* and *shahed* in
one verse:

No *shahed* that came to my sight (*nazar*) in coquetry
Could enter my heart for this is your place
[*Kolliyat*, p. 433.]

In this couplet the lover says that he does not disregard potential critics so they cannot catch him in *nazar-bazi* with the beloved. This is word play because *nazar-bazi* does not just mean looking or even the exchange of erotic looks, but also deeper involvement:

> I do not take my look (*nazar*) off the critics
> So they could not tell that I do *nazar-bazi* with you
> [*Kolliyat*, p. 558.]

In this couplet too, the first verse refers to the general love of youths, but the second is about the beloved looking at the lover:

> Never in my life will I be able to stop *nazar*
> Take not your *nazar* off me o' fount of beauty
> [*Kolliyat*, p. 524.]

The same interplay of words is observed in the following couplet:

> If *nazar* is a sin I have sinned many times
> I cannot stop myself from looking (*nazar*)
> [*Kolliyat*, p. 556.]

In the following couplet "shedding the people's blood" is a metaphor for breaking the heart of a lover:

> Those who declare *nazar* is a sin
> Do so by shedding the people's blood
> [*Kolliyat*, p. 539.]

In this couplet the composite word *sahab-nazar* is used in plural form, meaning those who admire youths:

> You rob sleep from the eyes of *sahab-nazaran*
> Worried that they would see your image in a dream
> [*Kolliyat*, p. 603.]

The same term is used in the following:

> Stop making fun, beloved, there are *sahab-nazaran*,
> Known and unknown, watching you from the front and back
> [*Kolliyat*, p. 500.]

There can be many more examples of the use of these terms that indicate the gender of the beloved. In the following the poet makes explicit the limits to which the love of the youth should go:

> Not every one can be said to be *sahab-nazar*
> Loving is one thing, carnal desire, another…
> Tell he who cannot bear the fire of his love
> Beware, it is wings that undo the moth…
> A human-being becomes human by shedding
> Passionate desire, or he is no more than an animal…
> All my life I will not drop these fetters which
> Put on my feet by you are like a crown on my head
> [*Kolliyat*, p. 436.]

GHAZALS ON HUMAN LOVE

As noted, apart from his ethical-mystical *ghazals,* which comprise ten percent of the total, Sa'di's *ghazals* may be divided between four categories: those which express love for the beloved; those which describe the beloved; those which express the joy of union; and those which reflect the sadness of separation. Inevitably, there is some overlapping among these four categories. Yet there is still enough distinction among them to justify such a grouping.

Whether in the expression of love, the description of the beloved or any other category of love poem for a human being, the same idealism mentioned above is the fundamental characteristic, not just of Sa'di but of all classical Persian poets from the twelfth and especially thirteenth century onwards when Sa'di flourished. Indeed it may be fairly claimed that Sa'di's love poems for human beings raise this classical genre to its level of perfection and are unsurpassed, if at all equalled, by the best of what came after him.

Love is virtually one-sided, the lover lacks an ego vis-à-vis the beloved, or his self is denied and annihilated into the beloved's supreme existence. There may be occasional complaints of the attitude and behaviour of the beloved: her lack of response to the poor lover's begging for her attention; her lofty inattention to the pain and suffering of the lover. But all such complaints are muted, qualified and sometimes regretted even in the same poem.

As noted, it is not difficult to see, or at least presume, the influence of mysticism and mystic love in this romantic idealization of the object of love and abject self-denial of the lover. Yet, at least as regards Sa'di's love poetry, matters do not simply stop at that. There is the obvious flesh and blood which the poet and lover sometimes manage to enjoy in carnal passion. We shall discuss this subject further when we come to read Sa'di's poetry on union with the beloved.

Expression of love

This group of Sa'di's *ghazals* describe and demonstrate the breadth and depth of the lover's love and desire for the beloved, occasionally but not often also describing some of the qualities of the beloved and some of the feelings of the lover when being alienated from her.

Love at the dawn of Resurrection
In this *ghazal* a remarkable theme has been used to express the heights of the lover's love for the beloved. There is no mention of the lover's love in the present life situation at all. It describes the lover's attitude towards the beloved at his death and, following that, at the dawn of Resurrection and into the other world. It thus implies and takes for granted the lover's total commitment and submission in this world and hence is an ingenious method of showing his selflessness towards the beloved at present.

> In the breath that I die, for you I'll be longing
> Hoping to turn into the dust of your belonging
> At the dawn of Resurrection when my eyes open
> For you I'll be looking, to you I'll be talking
> There will be gathered the beauties of both worlds
> Being a slave to your face, at you I'll be looking
> In the realm of nothingness a thousand years if I sleep
> I shall rise up in the end by the scent of your hair deep
> I will not speak of Eden or smell the paradise rose
> Or pursue the houris, to you I'll run without pause

I will not drink of Heaven's wine, ruby bright
I will not need it, being drunk by your sight…
[*Kolliyat*, p. 560.]

Self-effacing lover

The following *ghazal* is a perfect example of the lover's abject self-denial vis-à-vis the beloved. The lover declares that he is too little and humble to be the beloved's lover, or the lover is too exalted to pay any attention to his confessions of love. He is just a thorn to the beloved's rose, and could only rise up to the beloved's level if she herself casts "a ray of affection' on him. Yet the poet in the lover knows his own artistic value despite humbleness towards the beloved when he says that people love his poetry even though it is the beloved who inspires it.

Who am I, worthless me, to ask for your hand
It is unfair if I am your lover, you my beloved
I am not of a rank to rise up to your station
Unless I am elevated by a ray of your affection
I will not attach myself to you for I do not
Wish at all to be your thorn and you my bud
How could people not love hearing me
When I do so much love seeing thee? …
Your favours I'll not enjoy, I'll persist however
So I die in the process and become your creditor…
May Sa'di turn into dust if you do not like his body
I should not be proud of you and you ashamed of me
[*Kolliyat*, pp. 559–560.]

Come in peace tonight

Here, the lover had tried hard to avoid falling in love, but on seeing the beloved all his efforts proved futile. Not only did he lose his "reason" in the face of the beloved, but – as he begins the poem – he could not even keep his love a secret: "It was not possible to stop boiling on fire." The poem is impeccable but its highest effect is reached when the lover bids the beloved to go and see him at night: "Come to me today in peace tonight." He asks her to go in peace, which means to satisfy his desire. And he uses "today" in the sense of "this day," which also includes "tonight." In other words "Come to me this day, at night."

> I tried hard to hide the secret of love and desire
> It was not possible to stop boiling on fire
> I was alert from the start not to fall in love
> All reason faded seeing your face above
> Your mouth told the ears of my soul a story
> And now the people's warning is all a story
> Only you can stop the riot by hiding thy face
> I cannot give you up and turn away my face...
> Come to me today in peace tonight
> I have not slept longing for you all night
> You gave me up for nothing yet I am determined
> Not to sell a hair of yours for earth, sky and wind
> I'll mention my pain to someone who is wounded
> Telling a healthy person I would be reprimanded
> Do not say 'Sa'di give up love and passion'
> It will have no effect since I will not listen
> To enter a desert is better than remain inactive
> Even if I make it not I'll try to remain active
> [*Kolliyat*, pp. 560–561.]

The joy of loving and living

This poem describes the pain of loving but at the same time mentions the joy in loving and in suffering its pains, for which there is no remedy. One implies the other and he who has not experienced the pain cannot enjoy the joy. The lover is like a hunted animal entrapped in the beloved's lasso. It would be extraordinary for him to break out of it – to give up loving – but quite normal to die in captivity.

> The pain of love is one for which there is no remedy
> It is not strange if the painful moans of the tragedy
> People of reason know that those madly in love
> Listen not to the adviser and the preacher's advice
> He who has not drunk the wine of pain and loving
> Has not experienced the joy of loving and living...
> It is unusual for the game to break out of the lasso

But it is not unusual when it dies in the lasso
If the beloved knew what is happening to me
I would bear the cruelty of the rival and the enemy
My enemy's eye cried over my fate
The stranger sympathises but does not the friend...
[*Kolliyat*, p. 453.]

Descriptions of the beloved

The description of the beloved's physical attributes proceeds at the
same idealistic level as the expression of love. The beloved's physical appearance is perfect and in complete harmony according to the
contemporary aesthetic values. Her figure is often likened to a well-
proportioned cypress tree, her mouth to a flower bud, her body to
silk and silver, her hair to a long chain, and so on.

Body and soul
The beloved's face shines like the moon and her figure is as balanced as
the cypress tree. She is therefore more beautiful than both. Her lips are
sweet and her speech is sugar. Her face is like a perfect picture which, if
unveiled, would benefit the others without it being a loss to her. Swear-
ing at the lover is a generous act by the beloved that at the same time
makes him famous because his name has been mentioned by her.

My body and soul be a sacrifice to you beloved
I will not sell a hair of yours to the whole world
Sweeter than these lips I have not heard anybody
Speak, are you sugar itself or your mouth is honey
One day be kind and at me throw a dart
Luckily your hand and dart will be smart
Whether you turn back or cover your face
I will see the corner of your eye in the chase
The cypress tree lacks your moon-lit face
The moon has not your cypress-tree grace
Whoever blames us for loving you
Will take back the blame when seeing you
It is a waste your covering this picture of a face
Open, it profits the needy and costs you not a pittance

Come back, for in my eyes has remained your sight
Sit down, since your sign has settled in my mind…
Gracefully you swore at me, it made my fame
Happy is Sa'di now that you mentioned his name
[Kolliyat, pp.464–465.]

Site of Kaaba
The beloved is described as being no less than the site of Kaaba
around which he could run as they do in the rituals of Hajj. She is
a harvest of flower whose body is beyond description and is only
reflected by her garment; and the sun would be ashamed to set its
eyes on her. There is nothing in and about her that is not worthy of
praise, her figure, speech and movements.

You who have no pity for me at all
Blessed be your body and soul
What should I praise, your figure
Your movements or speech of sugar
Of your face must be ashamed the sun
When through the window it comes on
I shall not elaborate on your body
Your garment itself tells its story
You who are a harvest of flower
Give some to your flower's beggar
O' ravishing beauty try to be as kind
As your moral beauty would demand
O' site of the Kaaba show me a sign
So I can turn around you like a divine
Take my hand in the few days of this world
So I will not hold you to God in the next world
Out of my heart I intend to throw you whole
And instead give you an abode within my soul…
[Kolliyat, p. 463.]

Your naked body
The beloved's naked body is likened to a flower bed implying that
the lover has seen it. Her body is just like a soul hidden in the gar-

ment that covers it. She is so beautiful that seeing her beauty in the
mirror she is not likely to pay attention to the lover. The lover has
no remedy but despair, being so reduced by love-sickness that may
be blown by the wind at any moment.

> One with a figure of the cypress tree
> Is better than many real cypress trees
> How can one leave the beloved's side
> To go and watch jasmine and tulip aside?
> In the mirror, you never have seen
> As beautiful as yourself a scene
> Seeing just your own reflection
> How could you give me attention?
> The size of your mouth I will not mention
> It cannot even hold a word by intention
> Wrapped in the garment, your body
> Is just like a soul inside a body
> And he who would see you naked
> Would say it is just a flower bed...
> If the wind comes it will take me
> Sorrow has made it easy to break me
> The remedy o' Sa'di is despair
> When there is no remedy or repair
> [Kolliyat, p. 637.]

Union

Union and separation are the most prevalent themes in the classical
ghazal, one implying the other. *Vasl* literally means joining or attachment and, socially, the coming together of the lover and beloved. It
has a wide meaning, including being accepted and approved by the
beloved, getting back together after a period of alienation, seeing
each other again after physical separation, especially a journey, or
indeed being together in loving union. *Shab-e vasl*, the night of union,
would normally mean literally the night of getting together in the
bond of love, but it could also have a broader meaning including
seeing the beloved after a period of separation

Describing positive ideas and incidents is normally more difficult than negative ones, irrespective of the subject, just as it is easier to destroy than build. This is particularly true of writing on fulfilled love, on union, rather than on failed love, on separation, in classical Persian poetry, especially given the romantic and highly subjective context in which classical love and loving proceed. Sa'di is generally the undisputed master of writing *ghazals* on pure human love. But his genius shines particularly when he takes on the difficult task of writing on the lover's union with the beloved, which incidentally reflects a rich personal experience.

In the beloved's embrace

This *ghazal* is a gem. It is probably the best that Sa'di wrote on union, and possibly the best in classical Persian poetry on this subject. Putting aside the richness of the imagery and other literary devices, it is a most vivid, though still idealistic, description of a night being spent with the beloved. The lover is ready to die once his desire is fulfilled. The thirsty come to life, he says, at the sight of water; he is immersed in it and yet is thirstier. He would rather they made love in the garden but is worried that strangers, neighbours, would catch them and give them away: "If I did not mind the nightingale of the dawn." He uses the subtlest excuse for putting out the light, by "cutting off the tongue" of the candle so it could not tell others. He uses as subtle an excuse to take off his clothes "if it comes between us."

This one night in my beloved's embrace
If they put me on fire it will leave no trace
Once my desire is fulfilled death brings no fear
I am ready like a shield for the arrow of fate
O' heavens shut the window of the morning to the sun
Tonight I am happy with the moon as it shone
Is this the morning star or the Sacred Night
Is it you in front of me or just your thought?
I wish we could go and sleep out on the lawn
If I did not mind the nightingale of the dawn
These two eyes with which tonight I see you
Pity if I set them on someone else tomorrow

The soul of the thirsty is soothed by a river
In river I am drowned and still thirstier
Speak! There is no stranger except the candle
Whose tongue I will cut off this moment and handle
Nothing would separate us except this garment
And if it comes between us I will tear it apart
Do not say Sa'di will not survive this love
Say how I can shed the sadness of your love
[*Kolliyat*, pp. 553–554.]

The wonderful felicity

This *ghazal* also describes a night of union with the beloved. It is almost as rich as the previous one in the use of imagery and metaphor and as ecstatic in having the fortune of enjoying the beloved's presence. The lover is so overcome by joy that he cannot believe his luck, frequently wondering if the experience is real, not a case of hallucination. And the moment that he believes it to be true he wonders why he deserves such bliss.

God am I so fortunate that I see the beloved's face
Above her silvery figure a flower full of grace?
Did the heavenly tree grow in the garden of my soul
That in every branch I see a bird with a sweet call?
Has the world expired that so freely in paradise
I drink pure wine and see flowers thorn-less?
I am astonished at my luck and keep wondering
Am I drunk or asleep, or the beloved I am seeing
I have knelt and worshipped her many a time
Now I see her face and kiss her lips all the time
What good have I done to deserve such a reward?
What service have I performed to be lifted so upward?
Is it you beloved galloping towards me sleepily?
Is it me o' God being in so much luck so deeply?
Now that we are alone I do not want a candle
Being with her, paradise I do not wish to handle
What tulip did I smell that has perfumed my head?
What flowers should I bunch when the world is a flower bed?

I hear a voice saying what a wonderful felicity
That Sa'di is enjoying the beloved's company
[*Kolliyat*, pp. 568–569.]

Passion in place of love

This poem is once again on a night of union and complete fulfilment.
It somewhat goes further in that it explicitly mentions passion and
even puts it above love. It poses a very interesting and probably realistic contrast between love and passion, by the former meaning the
ideal of love, by the latter the desire of the flesh, even though the two
are connected: "When the passion of love arrived love gave in/To
rule the same kingdom, how can two shahs begin?" He cannot complain of the pain of separation now that he enjoys the joys of union,
and is happy to be perfectly alone with the beloved and wishes nothing to come between them. In a metaphorical allusion to Khosraw,
his beloved wife Shirin (Sweet) and his favourite Shekar (Sugar), he
says that they do not need a third party, even one such as Sugar, to
join their feast of loving.

> No-one will ever come between us tonight
> By the dust of your feet not a fluff will be in sight
> Throw off the headband of coquetry and pride
> Open the garment and let that cypress-tree outside
> Ask me not of the pain of separation in union
> Being so fulfilled there is no room to complain
> Do not put sugar and flower in our feast
> Shirin with Khosraw need Shekar in the least
> When the passion of love arrived love gave in
> To rule the same kingdom, how can two shahs begin?
> So full is Sa'di's head of music, song and gaiety
> No room is left for morals, ethics and piety
> [*Kolliyat*, p. 469.]

Separation

As noted above, this subject is generally easier to write on than is the union of lovers. In fact most classical love poems are about separation rather than union, mainly because it was a more frequent experience, but partly also because it was much more difficult to describe the joy of success. Sa'di's numerous love poems are not entirely crowded with songs of separation, but more particularly his poems on separation are not normally as hopeless and tragic as many such poems by others, for example Vahshi Bafqi's heart-rending, if a little too melodramatic, account of his "depression" and "disorientation." There is sadness, a sense of loneliness, sometimes alienation, in Sa'di's poetry of separation but seldom abject despair and depression. This too puts his love poetry to some extent apart from others who have written on the same theme.

A night of loneliness

This describes realistically the experience of going through the night totally absorbed and preoccupied by the beloved in her absence and probable lack of faith. It is a long night in which there is melancholic, anxious and uncontrolled thinking and so no chance at all of a wink of sleep. The morning is dragging and the dawn does not arrive both to lighten the dark and to make cocks and muezzin break the silence of the night. The poem finishes on a pessimistic note: "Sa'di's tears alas do not turn your heart of stone/Whereas a mill can turn by the water of my eye alone."

> The sun does not deign to rise this night
> What thoughts traversed the mind and no sleep in sight
> Why are you so late o' morning that I am about to fall
> You sinned and the muezzins failed to make their call
> The cock is choking just to try and crow once timed
> All the nightingales died and only the ravens survived
> The fragrance of the morning do you know why I love and chase?
> It looks like the beloved when the veil is removed from her face
> My head begs of God to fall down to her feet
> Since it is better to die in water than of thirst
> My guilt is not such that you deliver me to my enemy
> Do it by your own hands if you wish to torture me
> Sa'di's tears alas do not turn your heart of stone

Whereas a mill can turn by the water of my eye alone
Go off miserable beggar and find another door to solicit
Here you begged a thousand times and got no reply for it
[*Kolliyat*, p. 518.]

Farewell to the beloved

This *ghazal* is about physical separation, of saying farewell to a beloved
who is taking the caravan on a long medieval journey with little hope
of return. It is an example of expressing deep sadness without being
depressed, which ends with the realistic note that, however long it
may take, the sense of separation would eventually be forgotten.
Saying farewell to friends makes stones cry aloud. The lover is sob-
bing so hard, like a spring cloud, that the camel driver could use his
tears instead of storing rain water. It will be hard and long, yet it will
eventually pass: "Years have dug in such affection inside your heart/
Sa'di, that only years could remove from your heart."

Let me cry aloud like the spring cloud
Farewell to friends makes stones cry aloud
Anyone having once tasted the wine of separation
Knows the pains of loss of hope and aspiration
If you tell the camel-driver about the water in my eye
He would not put the water-skin out on the rainy day
They left us, eyes filled with the water of desire
Weeping like the sinful at Resurrection with Hellfire
O' morning of the night-dwellers I have lost
Patience that you are late like the night of those who fast
So much that I have said about your love's story
It is but one in a thousand of my grief and misery
Years have dug in such affection inside your heart
Sa'di, that only years could remove from your heart
I have told you enough, now I will be coy
The rest I shall tell those whose sympathy I enjoy
[*Kolliyat*, pp. 578–579.]

Anything but separation

Here, the beloved has broken her pledge and left the lover stranded, but there is clearly still hope, and in any case his world is apart from those who advise him against love and loving. He is prepared to give up anything but will not accept separation, even if it is a case of roaming around the beloved's home in a beggar's disguise: "Love, poverty, being caught and scolded/I can take it all smiling but not being separated."

> Little did I know that kindness and constancy you lack
> It is better not to pledge your love than do it and break
> He who tells me not to love the lovely of our times
> They are obviously apart, their world and ours
> That is not just a mole, a chin, a dishevelled long hair
> It's a secret of God, it ravished everyone's eager heart
> Take off the veil for the stranger will not see your face
> You are too big to be reflected in a small mirror case
> For fear of the rivals I cannot knock at your door
> But I can try to come to your neighbourhood as a beggar
> Love, poverty, being caught and scolded
> I can take it all smiling but not being separated
> I had promised to tell all my sorrows when you come
> What can I say since sorrows leave me as you come
> The candle should be taken and put out outside
> So the neighbours do not learn that you are inside
> Sa'di is not one who would break out of your chain
> He knows he is better your captive than free in pain
> [Kolliyat, p. 600.]

Some special features of the love poems

What follows is a short discussion of the aspects of Sa'di's *ghazals* which, at least in their frequent occurrence, are specific to his poetry.

Fetneh means both sedition and revolt. Sa'di attributes it frequently to the beloved and the consequences of her actions. Sometimes he calls her *fetneh*, meaning that she is the very essence of sedition: "Sit for a moment o' *fetneh* since chaos arose/*Fetneh* seldom settles when you are rising." And in another verse: "There must be a *fetneh* upon the roof/When someone's head is hitting the wall," it being the beloved on the roof for whom the lover hits his head against the wall of her house.

Often he refers to the onset ("rise") of revolt when the beloved rises, and its settlement when she sits down: "O' fire in the harvest of cherished people / Sit since a thousand *fetneh* has risen." In another verse he refers to chaos breaking out by the beloved's rising, and for "chaos" he uses the word *qiyamat* which also implies the act of rising: "Yesterday she reluctantly sat close to Sa'di / *Fetneh* subsided – *qiyamat* arose when she rose." In another verse he says that the seditious (*fattan*) eyes of the beloved are the sole cause of sedition (*fetneh*) in his homeland of Fars: "Sedition does not rise in Fars / Except by your seditious eyes." In this verse the poet says that when the beloved rises from sleep chaos rises a thousand times: "When your drunken eyes rise from sleep / A thousand *fetnehs* rise from all sides." Here are a few more examples of chaos and sedition, of making chaos and sedition, and of chaos and sedition rising:

I am so in love with your face that am not aware of myself
You are so seditious in yourself that are not aware of us
[*Kolliyat*, p. 545.]

*

Your eyes are the primeval magic
You are the eternal chaos
[*Kolliyat*, p. 638.]

*

I could not avoid chaos any more
As I got entangled with your seditious figure
[*Kolliyat*, p. 464.]

*

We had never heard of such a chaos rising
Stepping out of home and adorning the bazaar
[*Kolliyat*, p. 428.]

*

No sedition remained under this shah except Sa'di
Seduced by you as people are by his word
[*Kolliyat*, p. 531.]

Another aspect of Sa'di's love lyrics is the frequent use of the mirror: "Drop the veil for the stranger will not see your face / You are too big to show in a small mirror." Often it refers to the beloved seeing herself in a mirror: "Send for a mirror to see your own face / Your mouth will open up seeing your beauty." In the following verses the lover says that the beloved has not seen anyone as beautiful as herself except her own image in the mirror; and having done so she would not care to look at him:

> You who have never seen in the mirror
> Anyone as beautiful as yourself
> Seeing in the mirror one like yourself
> You will not look at one like me
> [*Kolliyat*, p. 637.]

The following verses are about the same theme:

> It is not amazing that you have bedazzled the world
> Seeing your image in the mirror you too are bedazzled
> With you wondering at your own beautiful face
> It is right that in your eyes, of us there is no trace
> [*Kolliyat*, p. 637.]

The following are a few more examples of the use of the mirror in Sa'di's love poems:

> The beauty of your perfect being cannot be described
> Only the mirror could tell the tale as perfectly as it is
> [*Kolliyat*, p. 467.]

> *

> No-one else is there to be loved like you
> Only in the mirror one sees one like you
> [*Kolliyat*, p. 267.]

> *

> If you see your own face
> You will be puzzled by your grace
> [*Kolliyat*, p. 467.]

> *

If looks in the mirror sink your heart
You will become incurably sick like me
[*Kolliyat*, p. 642.]

The contrast and conflict between love and reason are another feature of the poems. This is a familiar theme from mystic poetry but
rarely has it been used in the context of human love: "He is alert who
avoids loving, but/ My nature mingles not with reason. When the passion of love arose reason could not remain/ How could there be two
shahs in the same realm?" The following are a few more examples:

The army of love is looting reason, Sa'di
Stop believing that rational you may be
[*Kolliyat*, p. 561.]

*

Since the shape of your face overthrew reason
Love in Sa'di's mind may turn into madness
[*Kolliyat*, p. 509.]

*

Reason, even if it has a thousand arguments
Love claims it has the ability to refute them
[*Kolliyat*, p. 532.]

Reason is helpless in the prison of love
Like a Muslim in the hands of an infidel
[*Kolliyat*, p. 614.]

*

The rational person thinks and is cautious
Believe in love and be liberated from it all
[*Kolliyat*, p. 606.]

*

I asked love about the story of reason
It said it has been dismissed and holds no office
[*Kolliyat*, p. 455.]

*

Reason's and love's writs do not run in one place
There will be chaos in a realm with two rulers…
Ever since love stretched its hand to plunder
Reason proved unable to resist it and no wonder
[*Kolliyat*, p. 609.]

One recurring feature of the love poems is the fight between the lover and the beloved. But to call it "fight" is misleading because – contrary to the early classics – the lover and beloved are not equal here. It is the beloved who angers, leaves, fights, but the lover goes on loving her, declaring himself completely defenceless and ready to surrender:

Sa'di since her love is inevitable
Surrender and put your hope in fate
When she uses the sword, be the shield
Pray for her when she swears indeed
[*Kolliyat*, p. 585.]

*

If you use the sword I be the shield
There is peace on this side of the war
[*Kolliyat*, p. 644.]

*

If you attack using the arrow and the sword
We have no choice but to drop the shield
[*Kolliyat*, p. 581.]

*

You must be ready to drop the shield
When you fall in love with an archer
[*Kolliyat*, p. 525.]

*

Being in love with the bow of the beloved's eyebrows
Your life must be the shield when she rains arrows
[*Kolliyat*, p. 531.]

*

There is no choice but to drop the shield
The enemy has a stone and us a glass
[*Kolliyat*, p. 595.]

Sometimes the beloved "has gone in anger" and the lover begs her to
come back and kill him if she so wishes:

Take this message to the one who has gone in anger
Come back, we have dropped the shield if it is war
Kill us how you can for if we do not see you
The expanses of the world will feel narrow
[*Kolliyat*, p. 438.]

*

I wish she who has gone in anger would
Return – my hopeful eyes are fixed on the door
[*Kolliyat*, p. 435.]

Other examples directly refer to war and peace:

You who have raised the sword of unkindness on us
Peace we seek since we have no wish to fight you
[*Kolliyat*, p. 457.]

*

War or peace, it is your decision
We have surrendered our own will
[*Kolliyat*, p. 416.]

*

Remember that you were set on war?
The will is yours, whether peace or war…
Do what you will we wish not to fight, head down
Would be better where you have raised the sword
[*Kolliyat*, p. 608]

Another feature which anticipates Hafiz is critical remarks on the
"really existing" as opposed to ideal-type Sufis, and contrasts between
the lovers' attitude and theirs. Hafiz is famous for this but up till now
it has not been recognized that its original source is Sa'di's love poetry.

Even the term "libertine" or *rend*, which is a hallmark of Hafiz's *ghazals*, occurs in the love lyrics of his illustrious predecessor:

I am a servant of the joyous and libertines
Not the ascetics who regard you in secret
[*Kolliyat*, p. 465.]

*

I am a servant of libertines and selfless ones, who
In loving the beloved become their own enemy
[*Kolliyat*, p. 497.]

*

My beloved is a rogue a rascal a libertine
She pretends piety to herself and me
[*Kolliyat*, p. 499.]

The following references to the Sufis, *khaneqah*, tavern and libertinism closely anticipate Hafiz on such subjects:

It is past me friend to listen to advice
Go away jurist and do not sell us piety
[*Kolliyat*, p. 599.]

*

Go away learned doctor, leave us to the Almighty
Us, loving and drunkenness, you, prayer and piety
[*Kolliyat*, p. 606.]

*

Mohtaseb is chasing the libertines
Unawares of the *Shahedbaz* Sufis
[*Kolliyat*, p. 525.]

*

I cannot be patient seeing a pretty face
The Sufi would confess to his weakness
The poor man repented from seeing the beautiful
A hundred times, and will repent once again
[*Kolliyat*, p. 498.]

It takes much travel for a person to mature
Sufi will not purify unless he drinks wine
[*Kolliyat*, p. 634.]

Such is an account and a sample of Sa'di on human love, the true
expanses of which are vast, very artistic and highly exhilarating.[27]
But Sa'di also speaks on mystic love — apart from the ethical-cum-
mystical *ghazals* mentioned above — and compares and contrasts it
to the requirements of reason and science, and talks about genuine
and false Sufis and Sufi manners in *Bustan, Golestan* and elsewhere.
This is the topic of the next chapter.

4

REALITY AND APPEARANCE: MYSTICISM AND LOGIC[28]

Despite his universally acclaimed eloquence and clarity of expression, Sa'di's opinions, attitudes and ideas have been described in different, frequently conflicting, terms. He has been described as a sceptic, a pragmatist, a humanitarian, a moralist, an unethical writer, a religious preacher, and an Islamic mystic. Often, a combination of such attributes and appellations has been put forward by the same author and critic. The principal reason for this conflict of opinion is that it is virtually impossible to fit Sa'di's ideas into a system, a paradigm, a conceptual framework or school of thought, or easily locate him in a given category of classical Persian poets. In this chapter we shall first discuss Sa'di's relationship with Sufism, with reference to the views of major critics of his works, followed by a discussion of his views on Sufism and the Sufis directly from his prose and poetry.

RECEIVED OPINIONS

Sa'di's views on Sufism and Sufis appear to be fairly complex, although this apparent complexity would disappear if all aspects of the subject in his text were thoroughly studied. Reuben Levy wrote that Sa'di was "cast in a very different mould from Jalal al-Din Rumi's. His philosophy was much more practical and commonplace, and he was a stranger to metaphysics. He excelled in what are ordinarily called the Christian virtues: humility, charity, gentleness, and the like ... But he was no ascetic and he made no attempts to deny to others the earthly delights which doubtless he himself enjoyed."[29] Levy speculates about the possibility of Sa'di himself having travelled in the guise of a dervish and even having been initiated in a Sufi order, yet he says that "Sa'di never ventures ... to discuss Sufi doctrines with any thoroughness, and for that reason the point of his discourses is more easily and generally comprehensible."[30] Elsewhere, Levy contends that while Rumi was "reflecting on the mysteries of life and the oneness of the universe, the poet Sa'di was active distilling in verse the mundane experiences accumulated during many years of travel."[31] It is indicative of the complexity of Sa'di's views about this world and the next that while Levy describes *Bustan* as "an introduction to the whole range of mystic-ethical lore"[32] he goes on to say that "as in *Gulistan,* expediency is the main lesson taught," and yet he further adds that "the purely ethical spirit is not lacking, and approval is given to a wide and humane toleration."[33]

Jan Rypka's views are in a similar mould, and he surprises his readers by going as far as comparing *Bustan* with Keikavus ibn Eskandar's *Qabusnameh*. He describes Sa'di as being "less interested in abstract mystical speculation than in its application to everyday life, ethics and didactics."[34] Yet he maintains that *Bustan* is less of a didactic work than twelfth-century books in the genre, and that it looks more like *Qabusnameh*, a view which is hard to sustain in the face of the evidence. Edward Browne does not dwell on Sa'di's relationship with Sufism. He describes him as an "ethical" poet, but says that "in his work is matter for every taste...".[35]

Among the more recent critics Annmarie Schimmel quotes Herder describing Sa'di as "the pleasant teacher of morals," and Joseph von Hammer-Purgstall to the effect that Sa'di's "genius is less alien to the West than that of others, his imagination less overbearing." Schimmel's own comment is that Sa'di's "simple but elegant style, his practical wisdom, his charming anecdotes, made him a poet who appealed greatly to Europeans, especially during the Age of Reason, and has rightly been considered the Persian poet whose works is easiest for the Westerners to understand."[36]

Of the leading Iranian critics who have commented on the subject Badi' al-Zaman Foruzanfar has written about Shahab al-Din (Abu Hafs Omar ibn Mohammad) Sohravardi's possible influence on Sa'di's thoughts. He mentions five possible influences, two of which are particularly important for our subject. First is the view that as long as a practising mystic is still capable of describing his goal, efforts and experiences, he is still on the Way, for he who reaches the Goal completely breaks and loses contact with the mundane world. We shall come back to this point later in this chapter. The second influence of Sohravardi on Sa'di which Foruzanfar has suggested is that "Perfection is in following the Shari'a," i.e. that there cannot be true mystical experience outside the religious framework. He goes even further and says that, in general, Sa'di cannot be regarded as a follower of "the Sufi doctrine" because of his closeness to philosophers and men of politics on certain issues as well as the priority given by him to religious matters in certain respects.[37]

Zabihollah Safa's opinion is in keeping with that of Foruzanfar. He even emphasizes that Sa'di's education under Abolfaraj ibn Jawzi must have been "in religious sciences not in Sufism."[38] On the other hand Rashid Yasemi goes as far as claiming that the whole of Sa'di's love poetry – his *ghazal*s – have an esoteric meaning, and are of a wholly mystical nature – a view which, as noted in chapter 3, is very difficult to sustain against much of the evidence.[39] Ali Dashti's view is virtually completely opposite. He believes that the attribution of any degree of mysticism to Sa'di and his works is a mistake, which is in part due to Sa'di's association with one or two religiously inclined Sufis, and in part because of the existence of some mystical poetry among his *ghazal*s. But he fails to mention the considerable amount of material on and about Sufism and the Sufis in *Golestan* and especially *Bustan*.[40]

Finally, Ehsan Yarshater's recent comment synthesizes the conventional view in a consistent manner. Speaking about *Bustan* he remarks:

> Didactic in content, lyrical in tone, anecdotal in composition, this poem is one of the masterpieces of Persian literature. It is probably the best expression of humanitarian outlook on life and the moral dimensions that evolved in Islamic Persia among enlightened

preachers as well as a result of interaction between religious concepts and Sufi teachings; it embodies an ethical philosophy emphasizing moderation, justice, contentment, humility, detachment and compassion for the weak, and often draws on the lines and sayings of Islamic mystics to illustrate moral virtue. His humanitarianism however avoids the pantheistic and ecstatic excesses of some of the extreme Sufis. His approach remains of the application of ethical and devotional principles to common circumstances and problems. [41]

SUFISM IN SA'DI'S TIME

Islamic mysticism is almost as old as Islam itself. It was within the first century of the rise and spread of Islam that its mystical and esoteric interpretations began to emerge. Sufism in Iran dates back to the early centuries of the Arab and Islamic conquest, and mysticism in classical Persian literature emerges in the tenth (fourth *hijra*) and especially eleventh (fifth) centuries. The twelfth century produced two great mystic poets, Sana'i Ghaznavi and Attar Neishaburi, although mysticism was spreading fast and even literary poets like Nezami were not entirely untouched by it. In the thirteenth century it became dominant in attitude, approach and framework among intellectuals, as well as a way of life for many people, from all levels of society.

It is sometimes thought that the popularity of Sufism in the thirteenth century was due to the devastating Mongol invasions of Persia, especially the first wave which took place under Genghis Khan himself and wreaked havoc in most of the country. As noted in chapter 2, it was in this period and in response to the arrival of the Mongol hordes that Sa'di began to travel to the west. He wrote later in a poem:

When I came back the country was at peace
The wolves had shut their claws

Although modern historians have tended to doubt the scale of massacre and devastation as reported in Persian chronicles and other sources, there can be no doubt that the Mongol invasions were an abnormally devastating experience for many who lived in the thirteenth century. Sufism may have provided a refuge for many people who were struck by personal or social tragedy, insecurity and instability. Indeed some modern critics of Sufism such as Ahmad Kasravi almost believed that Sufism as a social phenomenon was a consequence of the Mongol invasions, and therefore a timid and ungallant response to upheaval and catastrophe. Others with a different social and psychological outlook may well regard this as a positive function served by Sufism at a time when individual gallantry was of very little consequence in improving the general situation, whereas mystic beliefs and values could help ease the worst of the calamities which faced both the individual and the society.

Just as it became popular among the people at large, Sufism also became a fashionable subject and creed among the elite, the thinkers, writers and poets, and even among the rulers and viziers who sometimes acted as patrons of Sufi individuals or communities. Both Rumi and Araqi among the thirteenth-century Persian poets were Sa'di's contemporaries, but the spread of mysticism even among the elite went far beyond poets and men of letters.

It was therefore inevitable that a leading writer, poet, thinker and social commentator such as Sa'di would take note of and respond to the great challenge of his time, not unlike the ideologies of the twentieth century, of which elites and intellectuals everywhere had to take notice and towards which they had to adopt an attitude, be it for, against or complex. As it happens, Sa'di seldom uses the term Sufi. As noted in the previous chapter, it occurs occasionally in his love poetry and is often not very complimentary, almost as if he is anticipating the downright negative attitude of Hafiz about Sufis, at a time when Sufism had become a firmly established if not orthodox tradition, and when more libertarian mystical approaches and attitudes had in the meantime sprung up.

Sa'di and Sufism

The three greatest bodies of work produced by Sa'di are *Bustan*, *Golestan* and his books of *ghazals*. Chapter three of *Bustan*, "Of Love,

Intoxication and Ecstasy," and chapter two of *Golestan*, "On Morals and Manners of Dervishes," almost exclusively concern Islamic mystics and mysticism, although these subjects are occasionally treated elsewhere in the two books as well. And we saw in chapter 3 that the large majority of Sa'di's *ghazal*s relate to mundane love, to love of the flesh. Only about ten per cent of the total is broadly mystical and/or didactic, yet a *ghazal* quite as intensely mystical in content as those of Rumi is hard to find among them.

Mysticism in Golestan

Chapter two of *Golestan* is the more empirical counterpart to the theoretical treatment of mystical themes in the third chapter of *Bustan*. On the face of it the attitude towards Sufism and the Sufis in *Golestan* would appear to be in conflict with *Bustan*, and since the two books were written one after the other, the apparent conflict over this and other matters between the two books cannot be attributed to a change of opinion. But in fact there is no real conflict between them. *Bustan* is, as noted in chapter 2, a somewhat theoretical treatise where ideal types are described, discussed and advocated. Even its first chapter, "On Justice, Sound Government and Good Judgement," contains counsel and admonition on the ideal management of the realm. And regarding Sufism and the Sufis too, as shall be noted, it deals with the ideal conception of Sufism and of the attitude and behaviour of the great Sufis, i.e. what mysticism and the mystics ought to be.

Golestan, on the other hand, is a more mundane and realistic work, dealing with similar topics and others as they exist in the real, generally imperfect, sometimes even grotesque world. The chapter on "The Morals of Dervishes," nevertheless, contains a critical assessment of Sufi practices which is both positive and negative, praising what may be termed as genuine or pure Sufi practices but rejecting impure morals and behaviour. It includes the shortest, most succinct and most eloquent definition of Islamic – perhaps all – mysticism in the following words: The appearance of dervishhood is ragged garment and shaven head. Its reality is a living heart and the ego dead.[42]

But this is followed by the remark that whatever a person's appearance, it is his piety, devotion and asceticism that reveal his true mystical commitments, castigating those who would use mystical beliefs as a pretext for indulging in frivolous living and libertine conduct.

Notwithstanding his clear and concise definition of "dervishhood," Sa'di is quite broad in his use of the term dervish, and he uses it interchangeably with *zahed*, *abed*, *parsa*, *saleh*, *aref* and *sheikh* to refer to anyone who practices a certain amount of asceticism, or who pretends to it. The general impression given by *Golestan* is that while he attaches great value to the heritage of the grand Sufis of the past, he is somewhat sceptical about the formalized mysticism of his own time. He writes: "They asked a Sheikh from Syria about the true meaning of Sufism. He said, 'In former days there was a group of men in the world, apparently distracted but in reality collected; now they are a crowd, apparently collected but in reality distracted'."[43] There are probably more instances of false or impure mysticism in *Golestan* than of the exalted morals and practises of venerable Sufis.

> An *abed* was sent for by a ruler. He thought to himself that if he took a drug to make him look weak and ascetic this would enhance the ruler's opinion of him. But it has been related that the drug was lethal and so he died in consequence of taking it:
>
> Who I saw all substance like a pistachio
> Was made of layers of skin like an onion
> Devotees who look towards the people
> Pray with their backs towards Mecca
> [*Kolliyat*, p. 79.]

Another *abed* was said to eat excessively in the evening and then continue to pray until dawn. An enlightened critic suggested that he would do better to eat less and sleep more.

> A *zahed* was a guest of a ruler. When they sat down to eat he ate less than was his habit, and when they rose up to pray, he prayed more than his wont, so that they would have a higher opinion of him:
>
> You will not make it to Mecca, o' Bedouin
> The road you are taking is to Turkistan

When he returned home he sent for food. He had an intelligent son. He said 'Father did you not eat at the Sultan's court?' He answered 'I did not eat enough in front of them'. The son said 'Then you should say your prayers again because what you did there would not be put to your credit':

You who display your virtues
On the palm of your hand
And hide your vices
Under your arm
What could you buy, o' arrogant fool,
In the day of need
With counterfeit money?
[*Kolliyat*, p. 73.]

A ruler told his vizier that he held two classes, the men of learning and the ascetic mystics, in great respect. "The philosophical, travelled and experienced vizier" (almost as if it was Sa'di himself) replied that in that case he should be kind enough to both groups by paying the former so they work harder, and not paying the latter so they remain ascetic.

On the other hand, genuine Sufis and dervishes are held in high esteem, and regarded as superior to the rich and mighty. It is true that, as noted in chapter 2, in the fictitious debate with the complaining dervish, the narrator takes the side of the well-to-do. But even there Sa'di's voice comes through the ruling of the judge who maintains that there may be good and bad within each group. Moreover, in a splendid description of the claim of dervishes vis-à-vis rulers he writes:

A certain ruler threw a contemptuous glance at a group of dervishes. One of the latter sensing the fact ... said 'O ruler, we are less than you in arms in this world present, but our life is more pleasant; at death we are your equal and will be better than you at Resurrection'...
[*Kolliyat*, p. 96.]

A ruler told a *parsa* 'Do you ever remember us?' He said 'Yes when I forget God':

Whom God rejects would run here and there
Whom He accepts has no need to go anywhere
[*Kolliyat*, p. 78.]

The same theme is expanded in another story, in chapter three of
Golestan, "On the Virtues of Contentment":

I have been told that a dervish was suffering from abject poverty, was
mending his robe and – to console himself – was saying:

To be content with dry bread and ragged clothes
Is better than to go under the obligation of others

Someone told him 'Why wait, because such and such a person has
a benevolent nature and a widespread beneficence ... If he learns
about your situation as it is he will regard it as an obligation to help a
worthy person.' He replied: 'Silence; it is better to die in need than to
take one's need to another person.'
[*Kolliyat*, p. 100.]

Mysticism in Bustan

Still, *Bustan*'s treatment of Sufis and Sufism is significantly more positive.
Being generally a more intellectual book, *Bustan*'s chapter three holds
some of Sa'di's more profound comments on mystic life and love, the
Seeker and the Sought. Elsewhere in the same book are some examples
of the approach, attitude and conduct of the legendary classical Sufis, all
of which are highly positive in tone. Shebli is said to have returned an ant
to its home after finding it in a sack of wheat which he had carried over
a long distance. Bayazid is quoted to have been thankful for someone
pouring a bucket of ash over him as he was leaving a public bath on the
Festival of Id, because he felt that he deserved (hell) fire and had only
received ashes. Joneyd is said to have shared his food with a toothless
dog while wondering which one of them was in fact better in the sight
of God. And alluding to such men, "the *abdal*," Sa'di says:

In ancient days, so it has been said
Stone would turn into silver in the hands of saints (*abdal*)
Do not think this report is unacceptable

When you are but content, silver and stone are the same
[*Kolliyat*, p. 339.]

Yet as noted before, it is in chapter three of *Bustan*, "On Love, Intoxication and Ecstasy," where Sufi ideas are put forward with full force and familiar authenticity:

Happy the days of those longing for Him
Whether they receive wounds or ointment from Him
Beggars they, having no love for kingship
Patient in their beggary in hope of Him...

Man's love of one like himself can be such as to make him forget everything but his beloved, let alone his love of the Eternal Source:

Given that Mundane Love, founded on passion
Is so potent and takes such hold
Is it surprising of the Seekers of Real Love
To be so deeply submerged in its ocean?
[*Kolliyat*, pp. 279–280.]

Almost the whole of this chapter of *Bustan* – together with the recurring mystical and esoteric concepts and imageries such as Beauty, Beloved, Seeker, Friend, Truth, Candle and Moth – may be cited as evidence both of Sa'di's familiarity with Sufi concepts and categories and of his great sympathy for, if not affinity with, those concepts. But he even surpasses himself when he contrasts love with intellect, and asserts that the intellectual approach to knowledge is nothing but "twists and turns":

The intellect is nothing but twists and turns
The mystics know nothing but God
One can say this to those who know the Truth
But followers of reason will [point to the facts of Appearance]
[*Kolliyat*, p. 290.]

To say that Sa'di has surpassed himself in placing mystical knowledge far above the logic of intellectual discovery is not to argue against the evidence, but to keep in view the fact that Sa'di's general regard for intellectual knowledge is high, and that in some places he regards it as being complementary to, not conflicting with, mystical knowledge. Yet it is worth noting that he regards some of the practicing mystics as unworthy of the ultimate goal of mystical discovery, and moreover, he who *is* worthy of it as unavailable to bear witness to it:

> These pretenders to being His Seekers have no news
> For he who heard the news ceased to be heard from
> [*Kolliyat*, p. 30.]

In other words, many a practising Sufi will not succeed, and the genuine mystics who do, remain unknown or will not speak of their knowledge:

> Lovers are killed by the Beloved
> [But] he who is killed cannot speak
> [*Kolliyat*, p. 29.]

The successful Seeker is not only one who denies himself carnal and material enjoyments but also one who asks for nothing in return. Here is an obvious contrast between the aims and objectives of the merely pious and the mystically pious, for the latter is ready to annihilate his body and soul, his entire being in any and all situations. "The pure wine of reunion is drunk/By he who forgets both worlds":

> If you are a man of Love take your piece
> Otherwise take the road to worldly peace
> Do not be afraid that Love will destroy you
> Since you will be eternal if it kills you…
> You will come to know the Truth
> Once you are liberated from your self
> For as long as you are with your self
> You will not reach inside yourself
> And this is a fact that is known
> Only by he who is without his self
> Not just music, even a beast walking
> Is musical if there is love and ecstasy
> A fly would not buzz at one ecstatic at heart
> Who would not start buzzing just like the fly
> The liberated knows neither bass nor tenor
> He would moan even at the song of a bird
> Never is the Singer without Song
> It is the ear that is not always open to sound

The last verse is a strange reminder of one by Rumi (a contemporary of Sa'di's whom the latter did not know but who might just have heard of Sa'di) in his Song of the Reed:

> My secret is not far from my moaning
> It is the eye and ear that lack the light

There follows a description of the music and dance sessions of dervishes, of their whirling until they become unconscious:

> When the ecstatic are worshipping Wine
> Listening to the music, they become drunk
> They begin to whirl just like the water wheel
> And weep down on themselves like the water wheel
> In Submission they sink into themselves
> And when they can no longer bear it
> They tear their garment into shreds
> Do not ill-speak of the drunken dervish
> He is drowning, hence he jumps and kicks

At this point Sa'di's virtually inevitable qualification occurs, his distinction between the false and true dervishes:

> I cannot tell you brother what music is
> Unless I know who the listener is
> If he flies from the Tower of Reality
> Not even an angel could keep pace with him
> But if he is a libertine, a licentious man
> Music will worsen his tendency to corruption...
> The world is full of music, intoxication and ecstasy
> But what can a blind man see in the mirror...?
> [*Kolliyat*, pp. 292–293.]

The above is a small sample of Sa'di's close understanding of the objects of mysticism and the methods of approaching them. It goes beyond a mere familiarity with basic Sufi tenets and – although perhaps deceptively – it conveys the impression that not only does the author himself uphold these ideals but that he has had some practical experience of Sufi living:

The selfless is a true lover
The selfish loves only himself
Since fate will one day take my life
I better be killed by the one I love
Human destiny ends up in death
Better then to die at the Beloved's hand
Since you will helplessly give up the ghost
Why not give it up at the Beloved's feet?
[*Kolliyat*, p. 295.]

The symbolic story of the candle and moth, though relatively short,
is a great poem and a masterly representation of mystical love and
self-annihilation. It does not seem to have been noticed by scholars
and critics that Attar Neishaburi has a *ghazal* on the same theme,
of which Sa'di may or may not have been aware,[44] but Sa'di's own
rendering in *Bustan*'s *mathnavi* is a masterpiece and probably the
best single poem in that book. One night the narrator listens to the
conversation of the moth and the candle. The moth tells the candle
that it is in love and so it is not surprising that it flies around the
candle in danger of being burnt. But it wonders why the candle, the
beloved, burns and weeps.

The candle replies that it weeps because it has been separated
from honey "my sweet beloved" (since candles were made from wax
extracted from natural honey). The candle reproaches the moth for not
observing that *it* is making the greatest sacrifice, not the moth, i.e. the
beloved makes an even greater and more selfless sacrifice and is more
completely consumed by the fire of love than is the lover: "You run
away from a single flame, raw/I am standing to be burnt head to toe":

One night I recall I lay awake
And heard the moth tell the candle
I am in love, I deserve to be burnt
But why do *you* so weep and burn?
The candle said 'O' my wretched lover
Honey left me, that sweet beloved...'
It was saying while the flood of pain
Ran fast down its yellow face:
'Love is not your way, o' pretender

> As you do not have patience or forbearance
> You run away from a single flame, raw
> I am standing to be burnt head to toe
> If your wings were burnt by love's flame
> From top to bottom it is putting me aflame
> The candle was speaking thus all night
> And the society was enjoying its light
> Suddenly after a while in the night
> A beauty present blew it out
> Its head in smoke, the candle said
> Of loving my friend, this is the end
> Do you wish to learn the art of loving?
> Die and you will be saved from burning
> Mourn not who has died by the Beloved's hand
> Rejoice, for the Beloved has taken him as friend
> [*Kolliyat*, pp. 295–296.]

Mysticism in other works

Reason and love, mysticism and logic, are also discussed in the five Homilies. There is some doubt on whether these Homilies belong to Sa'di or they have been added to his collected works afterwards. The reason for doubting their authenticity is simply that they do not exist in some of the earlier manuscripts. They are written in prose, and although they are not in the *mosajja'* style of *Golestan*, the language closely resembles Sa'di's writings. They contain the same duality of view which regards mystic devotion and religious piety as alternative, as well as complementary, approaches to knowledge and to salvation. Thus in the second Homily he writes:

> Know that piety is of two kinds: the piety of the Just (*salehan*) and the piety of the Mystics (*arefan*). The piety of the Just arises from their concern about the Day of Judgement in the future ... the piety of the Mystics, from the shame of the Lord of the Two Worlds at present...
> [*Kolliyat*, p. 899.]

And he goes on to add that knowledge of oneself leads one to the knowledge of God, referring to self-knowledge, which is the goal of mystic salvation as well as the cure for mental illnesses in modern psychoanalysis:

> Self-knowledge is the ladder for climbing up to the roof of the knowledge of God. How can he who does not know himself gain knowledge of the Sea of Glory … Whenever you get to know yourself you will get to know God. Your self is your key for getting to know Him.

God told Mohammad in the Qor'an to tell the faithful to explore the world, but scholars have interpreted this to mean the exploration of one's own world, "because if through the imagination you wander around the world of your own existence it would be better than if you travel the whole world on foot."

He writes in the third Homily that when Bayazid humbly prayed to God for a "drink of reunion" he heard a voice saying:

> Bayazid, your self is still with you. If you wish to reach us, leave your self at the gate and come in.

In the fourth Homily he tells us the story of the dervish who arrived at the palace of Ebrahim Adham, the ruler who later turned mystic and gave up his kingdom:

> One day Ebrahim Adham, God enlighten his grave, was sitting in front of his palace and his guards were in attendance. Suddenly a dervish arrived in rags and with a bundle and a stick, trying to enter the palace. The guards said 'Old man where are you going?' He said 'I am entering this caravanserai'. They said 'This is the palace of the ruler of Balkh'. He said 'This is a caravanserai'. Ebrahim ordered them to bring him forward. He said 'O' dervish, this is my palace not a caravanserai'. He said 'O' Ebrahim, whose was this palace first?' He said 'My grandfather's'. 'And after he died (?)', the dervish asked. He said 'It belonged to my father'. 'Whose did it become when your father died (?)', he asked. 'It became mine', he replied. 'To whom will it belong when you die (?)', the dervish asked again. 'It will belong to my son', he said. The dervish then said 'O' Ebrahim, where someone enters and another leaves is a caravanserai, not a palace.'
> [*Kolliyat*, pp. 907–908.]

He writes in the fifth Homily that someone went to Bayazid and having listed all the efforts which he had made, wondered when he might reach the Goal. Bayazid replied:

> Here are two steps. The first step is towards people; the second, towards God. Take a step from the people so as to reach God.
> [*Kolliyat*, p. 910.]

If there is any doubt about the authenticity of the Homilies, there is none about the essay on Reason and Love (*aql va eshq*). Sa'di wrote the essay in response to an admirer's request in verse to judge which of the two means of gaining knowledge has priority over the other. He replied in prose:

> Said the Messenger of God, God's blessing and peace be upon him, the first thing that God Almighty created was the intellect or reason … Therefore [the questioner's] logic is absolutely sound in bringing reason before love, and regarding it as means of getting close to God.

But, he goes on to add:

> Reason, although superior in many ways, is not the Way, but the light which shows the Way … And the use of a light is that, by means of it, they can tell the road from wilderness, good from evil, and enemy from friend. Yet a person with a light would not reach his destination unless he takes to the road.
> [*Kolliyat*, pp. 888–889.]

He goes on to explain that according to the great Sufis the seeker will reach a point that is hidden from intellectual knowledge. This claim would be excessive unless it was also made clear that intellectual knowledge is but a means of reaching the desired goal, not the goal itself. The seeker of the Way must acquire good morals through the intellect to enable him to purify his self. Self-purification will lead to isolation from others, and this will result in inner knowledge and the subjugation of his will. The process begins with the constant invocation of God's name (*zekr*), reaches ecstasy, "and the last stage which knows no end is called love."

Love, Perfection and Truth are like a great treasure. And just as kings destroy those who know the whereabouts of their treasure, so "the King of the Beginning spills the blood" of those few who acquire real knowledge of Him so that the story of the Treasure will not be retold:

> He who receives a cup in this feast/Is first made unconscious; so that the unknown secret of the essence of the Unique Being remains buried.
>
> [*Kolliyat*, p. 889.]

Therefore, although reason is necessary for guiding the Seeker to the right path, most seekers will not succeed because the trial is hard and requires a strong commitment, while those who reach the Goal are lost to humanity because they are then "killed" by the Beloved.

At this point, Sa'di's comparison in *Golestan* between the impact and consequences of the two alternative paths to knowledge is worth noting. He says in verse that someone left the *kaneqah* (the Sufis' retreat) and went to the *madreseh* (college of scholars), thus breaking his pledge to the People of the Way. Sa'di asked him what the difference was between the mystic and the scholar which made him choose the latter. He said: the former is trying to save himself whereas the latter is trying to save others. In other words, the end result of mystic knowledge is personal and individual, while that of intellectual knowledge is public and social.

CONCLUSION ON SA'DI AND SUFISM

Sa'di was a graduate of the Nezamiyeh College of Baghdad and hence a trained jurist, but did not remain in the *madreseh*. As noted in chapter 2 he comes close to saying that he escaped from scholasticism because of the rigid, repetitive and lifeless intellectual frameworks within which it proceeded. He was a moral theorist as well as a man of wide experience who combined his knowledge of theory and practice to produce some of the best didactic literature Persian language has known. He was also a man of public affairs who addressed rulers, ministers and public servants on the questions of just government and pious living, and occasionally praised them in verse, though this was normally moderate and was often combined with exhortations for fairness and tolerance. Judging by his lyrical poetry, he was, as noted in chapter 3, also a great admirer of youth and a lover of beauty who would both feel the happiness of the presence and the sadness of the absence of a human lover. Much of *Bustan* and *Golestan* concerns the application of broader ethical and social conduct. Excepting the one occasion in *Bustan*, cited above, Sa'di has a high regard for reason as a means of acquiring knowledge, and describes it as a light without which the path to mystic love would be hard to tread.

On the other hand his mystical compositions – especially but not exclusively in the third chapter of *Bustan* – are outstanding in depth as well as their degree of attachment to Sufi ideals. Indeed if this one chapter of his works alone had reached the modern reader, he would have been regarded as a classical mystic poet. Apart from that, he holds both here and elsewhere in saintly veneration the legacy, memory and legends of the grand old Sufis, and believes that a select few mystics may attain exalted degrees beyond the reach of ordinary mortals. However, he takes a critical view of the organized Sufi practice of his own time.

Taking his works as a whole it is clear that he simply does not accept that either intellect or emotion must be the sole channel through which veritable knowledge of reality may be acquired. In this he comes close to the Socratic realists who are neither rigid rationalists nor pure mystics, but admit that there may be various roads to knowledge. He once said in a *ghazal*:

> The whole of my clan were Doctors of Religion
> Your love as my teacher made me write poetry
> [*Kolliyat*, p. 423.]

If Rumi left the academy to become a poet and mystic, Sa'di left it to become a poet and lover. It is difficult to find in his work an ideological outlook, whether intellectual or mystical, despite his great knowledge of these fields and respect for them. And above it all, he remained a poet and lover.[45]

5

TEACHING MANNERS AND MORALS

There are few aspects of life on which Sa'di does not speak. In *Bustan* and *Golestan*, but also in some of his *ghazals*, *qasidehs* and other pieces which counsel and advise on private and social attitude and behaviour, he teaches morals and manners and advocates a model of good, clean, fair and considerate public and private conduct, which would afford its practitioner a healthy, contented as well as socially useful life in this world, and assure him a good place in the next.

In reviewing Sa'di's teachings two points should be borne in mind. One is his extraordinarily rich and varied personality and experiences: a poet; a lover; an admirer of mystical values; a doctor of contemporary sciences – including jurisprudence, theology and philosophy; a traveller in much of the then Islamic world; an acquaintance and occasional companion of rulers and viziers; and finally a venerable sage, not just of Shiraz but of Persian lands and beyond. It was a couple of decades after his death that Ibn Batuta, the well-known Tunisian traveller, observed the esteem in which Sa'di was being held in his home city. He also heard in China one of his *ghazals* being sung with a Chinese accent and without any knowledge of its meaning, except perhaps the reference in one of its verses to "the portrait artist of China."

The other point is his time and place. The thirteenth century was a very different age from our own, and even then things were considerably different between the world of Islam and that of Christian and feudal Europe. The question of "historical relativism" has been subject to controversy for ideological, political and moral reasons. Although the matter should be of mere scientific and philosophical interest, it tends to arouse emotional reactions sometimes even among scientists and philosophers. Its equivalent in our time is the concept of "cultural relativism" which gives rise to even more intense emotions, for example whether the criteria of human rights in a third world country should be judged by that particular county's cultural and religious norms or by the Universal Declaration of Human Rights.

Whatever the solution to such social and political controversies may be, it would be difficult to maintain that contemporary norms and values could be simply and without qualification used to judge ideas and events in the medieval period at any point on the globe. Echoing Vico, Isaiah Berlin went further and argued that it would be, if not virtually impossible, extremely difficult for us to arrive at a realistic understanding of ancient and classical cultures and civilizations. Instead of the concept of "historical relativism," he proposed that of "cultural pluralism."[46]

In the thirteenth century, Islam, in its variety of schools and sects, was the central religious and spiritual framework within which virtually everyone lived and died in Islamic countries. Government was not just absolute but also arbitrary, the word of the ruler being law as it had been since the foundation of ancient Persia. Early in the century Mongol hordes had overrun the country. In the middle of the century the second wave of Mongol invasion led by Hulagu Khan overthrew both the remnants of Persian Ismai'lis and the Abbasid caliphate in Baghdad, the latter in the same year that Sa'di wrote his *Golestan*. It did not take long for the autonomous government of Fars, Sa'di's homeland, with its capital Shiraz to fall effectively under the rule of the new Mongol Ilkhan empire which was centred in Azerbaijan. As noted in the previous chapter, it was an age in which Sufism became widespread among ordinary people and a definite subject of conviction and disputation within the elite.

Considering the time and place, and the social and cultural context, Sa'di comes through his preaching as a highly civilized man, even by today's standards. It would have been astonishing if he did not think that Islam was more righteous than Judaism and Christianity, although even here the references are very few and the sentiments not strong. What is very unusual is his religious tolerance if not relativism, for example in the story of the argument between the Jew and the Muslim noted in chapter 2, which could expose the author to the risk of excommunication even today in any orthodox situation.

EDUCATION AND EDIFICATION

Education in the wider sense of the term is a familiar theme both in *Bustan* and in *Golestan*. The title of chapter seven of *Bustan* is "On the Realm of Edification," and that of chapter seven of *Golestan* "On the Impact of Education." But the treatment of aspects of these topics is spread over many parts of both books. As it happens, there is a story in the first chapter of *Golestan*, "On the Manners of Rulers," which deals with the possible effects of education.

The story is about a group of highwaymen who had occupied a strategic position on top of a mountain and raided the caravans passing below. Their hideout was such that it was impossible to storm it with troops. In the end a few soldiers managed to smuggle themselves in while the robbers were out looting a caravan, and hid themselves in the cave. The robbers returned and "the first enemy that attacked them was sleep." The soldiers then fell on them, and captured and took them to the court. The ruler ordered their execution, but there was a youth in their midst who happened to be the son of the leader of the gang. A minister "kissed the threshold of the ruler's throne" and begged him to spare the boy's blood. The ruler did not like this intervention and said that to try and change this boy would be as futile as trying to keep a walnut on a dome:

> It would be better to put an end to their rotten generation and
> uproot their line, since no wise man would put out the fire but keep
> the spark, and kill a serpent but keep its offspring:
> Even if clouds rain down the Elixir of Life
> The willow tree will not bear any fruits

The minister listened to this "obediently but reluctantly" and said that the ruler was right on the assumption that the youth would continue

to live with the thieves, but he was hoping that in the company of good
men he would take the right path and learn to behave properly:

> Lot's wife befriended a bad lot
> She lost her saintly connection
> The dog of the Companions of the Cave
> Followed the good and turned human

The minister having said that, other notables joined in the plea until
the ruler reprieved the youth. He was put in opulent circumstances
and able teachers were employed to educate him. In time he was
well educated and everyone thought highly of him. One day the
minister gave an account of his progress to the ruler, but the latter
smiled and said:

> A Wolf's cub will one day become wolf
> Even if it is brought up by humans aloof

A couple of years later together with a gang of criminals he killed the
vizier and both his sons, robbed his home and took his father's place as
the gang leader in the same cave. When the ruler heard this he said:

> How can you make a good sword from bad iron (?)
> A nobody will not become somebody by education
> The rain, the softness of whose nature no one denies
> Grows thorn in the desert and tulips in the garden

And again:

> Flowers will not grow in the desert
> Waste not seed and effort in trying it
> Being good to he who is no good
> Is like being bad to one who is good
> [*Kolliyat*, pp. 40–42.]

On the surface it looks as if the question is one of "nature versus
nurture," and that the story's conclusion is that goodness is hereditary and cannot be acquired by good upbringing. In fact, it is more
complex. The story does not deny the effectiveness of formal education, since the youth learned all that he had been formally taught
and became an accomplished young man. The fact that he turned

out to be a criminal nevertheless was either for hereditary reasons or simply because he had grown up with criminals and had been a young criminal himself. It is not clear from the story which of these was the reason for his reversion to the old ways.

The effect of formal education, on the other hand, is dependent on the person's level of intelligence and intellectual potential, which, to a considerable extent, may be hereditary. In chapter seven of *Golestan*, "On the Effects of Education," we read that a certain vizier "had an unintelligent son." He sent him to a learned man and asked him to instruct the boy "so he may gain intellect." But a period of instruction proved ineffective and the learned man told the boy's father that "he does not gain intellect and is making me go mad":

> When someone's nature is receptive
> Education will have an effect on him
> No amount of polish will improve iron
> Which is fundamentally rotten
> Wash a dog in seven seas and it gets
> [Ritually] more unclean by getting wet
> If they take to Mecca the ass of Jesus
> It will still be a donkey when it returns
> [*Kolliyat*, p. 153.]

Another story along the same lines and in the same chapter tells of a ruler who sent his son to a man of learning to bring him up with his own sons. The learned man agreed but no matter how much he tried the boy did not succeed, whereas his own sons acquired much knowledge and intellectual virtue. When the ruler complained to him, thinking that he had not sufficiently taught and instructed his son, he replied that "the education is the same but the natures are different."[47]

The upshot is that formal education will not change a person's basic character regardless of whether it has been formed by hereditary or environmental factors, or indeed a mixture of the two. Furthermore, the extent to which education will result in the acquisition of knowledge and manners depends on the pupil's intelligence, and this is not determined by "blood," or the son of the ruler would have performed as well as the teacher's sons.

But to gain knowledge and learn manners is no guarantee that they would be put to good use. A century before Sa'di, Sana'i Ghaznavi compared a learned crook to a thief who is using a lamp: "When a burglar comes with a lamp he chooses the best items." Sa'di writes:

> Two people laboured in vain and endeavoured uselessly: he who accumulated and did not eat, and he who learned and did not practise.

He adds that "he who learns and behaves ill is like a blind man carrying a torch." And further: "Three things will not last, wealth that is not used in trade, knowledge that is not subjected to debate, and government that lacks punishment":

> An uneducated and ignorant commoner is better
> Than the learned man who uses not his knowledge
> The former goes off the road because he is blind
> The latter has two eyes and yet falls down the wedge

> 'Someone was asked what is analogous to knowledge without practice? He said, a bee that does not make honey':

> Tell the horrid bumble bee
> 'Kindly stop stinging
> Now that you do not make honey'

> 'Two men died regretting their life: he who was well off but did not eat, and he who knew but did not use his knowledge.'[48]

MORALS

Morals and manners may be learnt but are not necessarily the results of formal education. More often they are related to upbringing in the wider sense of the term, to the personality of the individual and to social norms and mores. *Golestan* and *Bustan* contain a great deal of instruction and admonition regarding what may be described as "good manners and moral behaviour," for fairness, moderation, contentment, charity and humility, and against jealousy, backbiting, meanness and greed. These ideals are more or less the same as those that are still preached in our own time, although the stories and anecdotes which Sa'di uses to advance them directly or indirectly are often outmoded and time-bound.

Charitableness

A whole chapter of *Bustan* is "On Beneficence," but Sa'di's advocacy of charity goes beyond mere recommendation of material help to the needy. It also encompasses a wide range of moral and spiritual generosity, even self-sacrifice, towards one's fellow human beings. There are two stories about Hatam Ta'i, the legendary Arab noble-man of the Tay tribe. He is believed to have flourished just before the advent of Islam and was praised by the prophet Mohammad because of his extraordinary charitableness and generosity. According to the first story Hatam had an Arab stallion which was unique in strength, stamina and speed:

> Swift as the wind, loud as thunder
> It overtook lightning and did wonder
> At its gallop rained dews on the plane
> As if April clouds passed in its wake
> Like a flood running through the desert
> The wind falling behind it like dust

The Sultan of Rum was told both about Hatam's great generosity and the uniqueness of this horse in his stables. He decided to test the legend about him and send a delegation to ask for his horse:

> To the wise minister the shah said
> Claims without proof are better not made
> I shall ask Hatam for that Arab horse
> If he was generous and agreed with this course
> He would show the glory of being great
> Otherwise he is just like wind in the air

The delegation arrived at Hatam's camp in the evening. He gave them "gold and sugar" and had a horse killed for feeding them. Next morning he was told about their mission:

> Hatam responded sad and melancholy
> Biting his hand remorsefully

Why did you, good sirs, he asked
Not give me the message at times passed
For I had that wind-like swift stallion
Last night grilled to feed you gentlemen
For I knew that because of flooding and rain
We could not reach the meadows in the terrain
I had no other way of feeding you
Only the stallion was here for treating you
[*Kolliyat*, pp. 267–268.]

We observe here that Hatam's generosity goes far beyond an ordinary act of beneficence. If he had just given them the horse it would
have been an act of considerable sacrifice, but one which would have
been publicly acknowledged. Apart from that, his dear and extraordinary horse would have been alive even though it would have been
in someone else's possession. But he sacrificed his horse for feeding
guests without being asked to do so, not suspecting that his great
sacrifice would be publicly known.

The next story about Hatam's generosity of spirit goes even further as Sa'di himself points out. A ruler in Yemen was known to be
extremely generous: "You could call him the cloud of beneficence/
Since gold rained from his presence." Once in a feast thrown by him
someone began to speak about Hatam and someone else added his
voice in his praise. The ruler became jealous and decided to have
Hatam killed, thinking that as long as Hatam was alive he would not
enjoy a unique reputation in generosity. He therefore sent someone
to find Hatam and kill him. When the assassin reached Tay territory
he met a man who acted as his host for the night and was so kind that
he made a very good impression on him. At dawn the host begged the
guest to stay for a few days longer. He replied that he could not because
he had a great mission. The host told him that if he would confide in
him he would try and help him in any way he could. He replied:

Have you heard of Hatam in this land
Who is high-spirited and well-intentioned?
The ruler of Yemen has asked for his head
I do not know what hostility lies behind it
All I ask you to do my friend
Is to guide me to find his abode

And here is he climax of the story:

> 'I am Hatam', the man laughed and said
> 'Just this moment cut off my head
> For when the morning light is effected
> You will be hurt or disappointed'

The would-be assassin was completely disarmed. He fell on his knees and said that he could not even throw a flower at Hatam let alone kill him. He went back to Yemen and the ruler "read in his face" that he had not fulfilled his mission. The assassin told him the story. The ruler was full of admiration for Hatam and gave the man a gift of money.[49]

In *Golestan* there is a story of a different kind about Hatam:

> They asked Hatam Ta'i if he had seen anyone with greater spirit than himself anywhere in the world. He said: Yes, one day I had thrown a feast for Arab leaders and sacrificed forty camels. Then I went to the edge of a desert to see to a need and saw a man gathering thorns and thistles. I told him 'Why don't you go to Hatam's reception as a whole crowd have gathered round his feast'. He said:
>
> Who earns his bread by his own action
> Will not go under Hatam's obligation
> I found him superior to me in greatness of spirit
> [*Kolliyat*, p. 105.]

There is a story about Abraham in *Bustan* which once again goes beyond the question of ordinary generosity and has long been known in the west as a model for religious tolerance. It had a great impact when it was first translated and has been cited as evidence of Sa'di's "humanism."[50] Once, a week went by when not one needy guest arrived at Abraham's "guest house," i.e. his home. He was so kind that he did not have his own meal on time and went and searched the desert looking for a guest. There he found an old man and most affectionately invited him to dinner. The old man accepted the invitation. But when, together with other members of the household, they sat around the spread on which the meal was served the old man refused to repeat the grace ("In the name of God ...") before starting to eat. It turned out that he was a "fire-worshipper." Abraham turned him out, and then:

Abraham heard God Almighty speak
Severely chastising him, saying
'A hundred years I gave him life and meals
And you hated him in a moment of unease
If he prostrates himself before fire
Why should you of your kindness tire?'

The story concludes that kindness and beneficence must be uncondi-
tional and no qualification should be required for extending them.[51]

The following story is in the second chapter of *Golestan*, "On the
Ways of Dervishes":

A burglar entered the home of an ascetic. The more he looked for
goods the less he found any. He was upset. The ascetic realized and
threw the klim on which he was sleeping in the burglar's way so he
would not be disappointed:

I have heard say that the men of God
Do not make unhappy their enemies
How could you ever attain their ways
When you make war with your friends?

The friendship of the pure is the same in one's face and behind one's
back. They do not criticise you in your absence and die for you in
your presence:

Before you, like a peaceable sheep
Behind you, like a man-eating wolf
*
Who mentions to you the fault of others
Will talk about your faults to others
[*Kolliyat*, p. 71.]

Also in *Golestan* is the story of a burglar who stole something from
a dervish. The judge ruled that they cut off his hand. The dervish
pleaded for him and said that he had no complaint. The judge said
that nevertheless he had committed a crime and must be punished.
The dervish said that what little he owned was in the nature of public
endowment (*vaqf*) and taking from an endowment was not a crime.
The judge let the burglar go but rebuked him for stealing from a

man such as the dervish. The burglar replied that he was the man worth stealing from.[52]

The following story in *Bustan*'s second chapter, "On Beneficence," is another example of the greatness of heart and spirit, beyond mere material help to others:

> Once a woman begged her husband to stop
> Buying bread from their local shop
> 'Go and shop in the corn market
> He does not seem to be straight
> Because his customers are few
> But for chasing flies he has nothing to do'
> To comfort her, the husband, who shopped in the shop
> Said 'O' light of our home, please accept and put up
> He set up shop here looking to us as customers
> It will be unchivalrous to deny him our purchases'
> Take the road of those who are liberated
> Now you are on your feet hold the downtrodden
> Be generous since the men of God
> Buy in shops which are not on top
> [*Kolliyat*, p. 259.]

A big-hearted and generous man did not have much money. Someone who was in jail for failure to pay a debt wrote and asked him to put up a small amount of money so they would free him from prison. The good man did not have the money, so he asked the man's creditors to let him go upon his guarantee to deliver him on demand. They agreed and let him go. The good man then went and told the prisoner to run away from town:

> He went to the prisoner and said
> Run away from town fast as a bird
> Like a sparrow whose cage is opened
> He did not remain in jail for one moment
> Like the morning breeze he left the land
> So swiftly that the wind was left behind
> They then seized the good man
> To deliver the money or the man...
> They say he remained in jail for some time

And neither complained nor made a fuss
Times passed and he had sleepless nights
A pious man went to see him and asked
I am sure you are not in others' debt
How then did you find yourself in jail?...
He said I saw a poor man weary of fetters
I could only save him by taking his place
I did not regard it to be just and fair
I being free and he being in jail
[*Kolliyat*, p. 261.]

Still in the same chapter of *Bustan*, Sa'di says that once he saw a young man with a sheep running after him. He told him that it is the leash that makes the sheep follow him. Immediately he unleashed the sheep and began to run, with the sheep freely running after him. Afterwards the young man returned to him and said it was not the leash that brought the sheep with him but kindness which was just like a leash on its neck. The narrator concludes that one should display kindness even to bad people:

Be kind to the bad, o' good man
A dog would be grateful if you fed it
A dog's teeth will not bite a person
Whose cheese the dog has eaten
[*Kolliyat*, p. 265.]

Someone's donkey had fallen in a ditch of mud in the desert at night during a storm. In despair, he began to swear at any and every person, including the lord of the land. The ruler happened to be passing by and heard all the invectives hurled at him. Someone told him to kill the unfortunate man, but he looked, saw him in dire straits, forgave him, and gave him gifts as well:

A man's ass had fallen into a ditch of mud
Its worry had brought to boil his blood
In the desert, with cold, rain and flood
Darkness had fallen on flood and mud
All night long until the sun rose
He cursed and swore without pause

His tongue spared none, enemy or friend
Not even the sultan who owned the land
By chance the lord of that vast territory
Was passing by and found it unseemly
He heard those unwise words and unkind
Neither could he bear to listen nor respond
He looked at his guards with embarrassment
Wondering at the man's words of harassment
A guard told him to raise the sword on the man
Who swore at everyone's daughters and women
The exalted sultan looked and found
That he was in trouble, his ass in mud
He forgave the poor man's transgression
Suppressing his anger at his indiscretion
He gave him money, horse and garment
How nice is kindness instead of punishment
Someone said 'You old stupid fool
You were very lucky', he said 'cool
If I mourned on account of my pain
He was generous in his own vein'
It is easy to wrong in response to a wrong
A good man is good to one who does wrong
[*Kolliyat*, p. 271.]

Someone found a dog in a desert dying of thirst. He turned his hat into a bowl, filled it with water in a well and let the dog drink from it. The Prophet heard about it and said that God had forgiven all of the man's sins. It is important to note that dogs in Islam are ritually unclean:

Someone found a thirsty dog in the desert
Barely alive, incapable of effort
The good man turned his hat into a bowl
And fastened his head-dress to it like a rope
He set to serve the dog and opened his arms
Thus did he gave water to the disabled dog
The Prophet informed people of his position
That the Judge forgave all of his transgressions
If you happen to be unkind think more
Try to be kind and put beneficence fore

Not even to the dog was kindness lost
How could it be lost to a man, robust?
Be kind and generous as much as you can
God has shut off charitableness to no man...
Many a powerful person fell from power
Many a downtrodden got their desire
Do not break the heart of the meek
One day you too may become weak
[*Kolliyat*, p. 262.]

Humility

Of the maxims of proper conduct and good behaviour which Sa'di
advocates, humility is one of those which top the list. In his works
humility, modesty and humble behaviour are part of a general maxim
of a good relationship with one's fellow human beings. He has spared
no word, anecdote or story to emphasize the importance, even
necessity, of this maxim. Not only does he believe it to be morally
just and socially desirable, but he says on a number of occasions that
humility is a winner, and will bring good to the person in question
as well as his associates. He does however also make the point that
too much humility displayed towards bullies would be interpreted
as a sign of weakness and should be avoided.

A long chapter in *Bustan*, "On Humility," is devoted to this subject, although in this case too the subject is occasionally treated
elsewhere in the book and also in *Golestan*. Here is the preamble to
the chapter:

Pure God created you from dust
Be humble like dust, you must
Be not greedy, offensive and dire
You were made of dust, be not fire
When the fire was rebellious [at Creation]
Dust instead put itself in a humble station
Since that was proud and this humble
They made humans of dust and demons of fire

*

A drop of water dropped down with the rain
It felt small seeing the breadth of the ocean
Thinking 'Who am I where is the sea
Where there is sea I might as well not be'
Since it showed modesty, the mother of pearl
Held it in its bosom and raised it as pearl
It was elevated to such an extent
That it turned into a glittering jewel
It rose high because it showed humility
It began to exist by pretending to nullity
In the very intelligent humility is found
A branch heavy with fruit lies on the ground
[*Kolliyat*, p. 297.]

In *Golestan* there is the allegorical story in verse of the debate between the curtain and the flag. The flag complains to the curtain that while they both serve the sultan, the curtain is in the company of nice and pretty servants, whereas it, the flag, spends all its time on the move, being carried by soldiers, and being exposed to dust and wind. It claims that it works harder and takes more trouble in its services and yet the curtain has a much better time without taking one step out. The curtain replies:

My head is at the threshold
Yours is up in the clouds
Whoever raises his neck high
Would fall on his neck from the sky
[*Kolliyat*, p. 94.]

Even when one is wronged one should respond to the wrongdoer with forgiveness and generosity. This is perhaps the most well-known Christian virtue, although its source in Sa'di is more likely to be classical mystic teachings, although it must be mentioned that Sa'di is not always consistent on this point. He says in *Golestan*:

I complained to a sage that a person has accused me of immorality. He said, 'Embarrass him by responding kindly:

Behave well so that the maligner
Cannot point to your failures

If properly tuned is the lyre
It will not be corrected by its player'
[*Kolliyat*, p. 83.]

There are stories on the same theme also in *Bustan*. For example,
a drunkard beat up a good man. Someone told him that he should
retaliate since "forbearance should not be extended to this ignora-
mus." He said a drunk would attack people, but a wise and intelligent
man should not attack an ignorant drunkard:

The mature person lives with kindness
He responds with kindness to unkindness
[*Kolliyat*, pp. 306–307.]

There follows immediately the story of the dog that bit the leg of a
desert dweller, which shifts the point from humans to animals. All
night the victim cried and moaned in pain. His little girl scolded
him for not having retaliated. He replied that he too had teeth but
he would never bite a dog's foot:

Even if they hit my head by a sword
I will never put bite a dog's leg
[*Kolliyat*, p. 307.]

There is a long story in chapter four of *Bustan* of a sinful man in the
time of Christ, which may be regarded as even stronger evidence for
Sa'di's "humanism" than what has been cited so far. "He was worse
than the devil. There was not the slightest good in him and his ways.
One day he watched a desert-dwelling ascetic pay homage to Jesus
and was moved by the scene. He fell on his knees, broke down and
repented of all the sins he had committed." The ascetic was terribly
annoyed that such a sinner had approached and addressed him:

What good has come of his sinful self
To wish to talk to Christ and myself?...
I am hurt by his unpleasant face
Lest his fire will affect my case
In the Day of Judgement, when they all gather
O' God keep him apart from me for ever

God spoke to Jesus and expressed His utter displeasure at the ascetic man's attitude. He said that the sinner had come to Him begging for forgiveness. He had not only forgiven him but will send him to Heaven:

> And if the ascetic man distains
> To sit with him in paradise
> Tell him not to be ashamed of him there
> He will be sent to Heaven, the ascetic to Hell
> [*Kolliyat*, pp. 299–301.]

And this price the proud ascetic paid for his lack of humility.

Contentment

Sa'di does not always advocate a totally ascetic life, and when he does he regards it as an ideal state achieved only by the select few, the true mystics. His advocacy of contentment does not discourage activity and effort to earn one's living, but criticizes greed and an obsession with material possessions, as well as a dependency upon others for the sake of enjoying a better material life. Chapter six of *Bustan*, "On Contentment," opens with the following verses:

> He did not know and obey God
> Who was not content with his lot
> Let the greedy who travels the world
> Know that contentment enriches us all
> [*Kolliyat*, p. 333.]

The ruler of Khotan gave an enlightened man a silk robe. He thanked the prince profusely but added that his own coat was better:

> The Amir of Khotan once did
> Give an enlightened man a robe of silk
> He laughed like rose leaves, red
> Kissed his hand, wore the robe and said
> How nice is the gift of The Shah of Khotan
> But one's own coat is better than that
> [*Kolliyat*, p. 337.]

In chapter 4 mention was made of the poem citing the legend that the great classic Sufis turned stone into money, which is followed by the comment that this is not incredible since money and stone are the same to a contented person. The poem continues in the following verses:

> Tell the dervish who worships sultans
> That the sultan is needier than a dervish
> A drachma will satisfy the beggar's hunger
> Fereydun owned Persia and still hungered
> A great burden is the management of a realm
> A beggar is shah, let them call him beggar
> A beggar who is not bound by worries
> Is better off than the shah who worries
> The peasant and his wife sleep in their place
> So well that the sultan cannot in his palace
> Whether one is a shah or a cobbler
> His night is still followed by the day
> When the flood of sleep carries you unaware
> The ground and the sultan's bed are the same
> When you see the rich full of arrogance
> Try to thank God o' impecunious man
> That you do not have the slightest power
> To be able to hurt and injure another
> [Kolliyat, p. 339.]

The natural inability to hurt other human beings as a gift of God is mentioned elsewhere in Sa'di's works. In chapter three of Golestan, "On Contentment," the story is told of two Egyptian princes, one who became ruler and the other a learned man. The one who had become ruler once spoke with contempt about the other, saying that he had inherited the realm whereas his brother lived in poverty. The latter replied that he was grateful to God who had given him the heritage of the prophets, learning, not the heritage of the pharaohs, the kingdom of Egypt:

> I am the ant that is trampled under foot
> Not the wasp that makes people moan
> How could I ever count the blessing
> That I lack the force to hurt other beings?
> [Kolliyat, p. 99.]

In the same chapter of *Golestan* there is the short account of an apparently personal experience:

> I had never complained of life and frowned upon destiny except when
> I was bare-foot and could not afford to have shoes. I reached the
> Friday Mosque of Kufa, unhappy. I saw someone who did not have
> legs. I thanked God for his blessing and put up with being bare-foot:
>
> Roasted chicken in the eyes of the well-fed
> Is worse than leeks on the dinner spread
> To he who lacks money and possessions
> Boiled turnips look like roasted chicken
> [*Kolliyat*, p. 107.]

And again in the same chapter:

> I saw a fat idiot, dressed in an expensive robe, riding an Arab stallion,
> and wearing a head-dress made of fine Egyptian linen. Someone
> asked: 'Sa'di, what do you make of this painted silk on this ignorant
> beast?' I said: 'It is an ugly script written in gold ink':
>
> An ass looking like humans
> A calf, sounding like an ox
>
> A fine creation is better than a thousand silk robes:
>
> You cannot say this animal resembles humans
> Except his cloak, turban and outward appearance
> Search among his things, possessions and existence
> You will find nothing lawful to take but his blood
> [*Kolliyat*, p. 112.]

The advocacy of contentment is not intended as encouragement of idleness or inactivity. This is pointed out in various places in *Bustan* and *Golestan*. In the former we read the story of how a disabled fox received his food, and this led a human observer into error:

> A person saw a handless and legless fox
> And was intrigued by the greatness of God
> Wondering how the fox managed to live
> How did it eat without hands and legs?
> He was deep in puzzlement that behold

A lion appeared with a jackal in its hand
The lion ate of the jackal as much as it wanted
The fox ate what was left of the jackal hunted

Next day he saw the fox receiving its meal again in a miraculous way. And so:

The man took faith in what he had seen
On the Creator he thought he must lean:
'From now on I shall be content like an ant
By its own will manages not even an elephant'
Head down, he stopped effort for a while
Awaiting God's donation from on high
Neither friend cared for him or stranger
He became just skin on bone from hunger
When he was weak and conscious no longer
He heard a voice coming from the altar
'Behave like a strong lion, o' rogue
Do not lie down like a crippled fox
Try to leave leftovers like a lion
Why be happy with leftovers like the fox?
He who has a thick neck like a lion is worse
Than a dog, if he behaves like a fallen fox
Earn your living and share it with others
Instead of hoping to receive from others...'
[*Kolliyat*, pp. 265–266.]

Jealousy and backbiting

Jealousy and backbiting have been roundly condemned in various stories and pronouncements both in *Bustan* and *Golestan*: "Passion, greed, grudges and jealousy are/Blood in your veins and soul in your body." In chapter seven of *Bustan* Sa'di tells the following story, apparently from his personal experience. It combines, in an artful way, a rejection of both jealousy and backbiting within the same metaphor:

I was a scholar in Nezamiyeh College
Searching day and night for knowledge
Once I told my master 'o' wise man

Such and such friend is jealous of me'
When the master of manners heard this
He was much annoyed and said 'alas!
You disapprove of your friend being jealous
What makes you think that backbiting is good?
If he took the road to Hell by his meanness
You will join him via another route like this'
[*Kolliyat*, p. 350.]

This is followed by another poem, forbidding backbiting even against
Hajjaj ibn Yusuf, the pitiless Umayyad governor of Iraq and Iran:

Someone said Hajjaj is a blood-sucker
His heart is as hard as a black stone
He does not mind the people's sighs
O' God avenge the people on him
An old and experienced man at once
Gave him an experienced man's advice...
Leave him and his life alone, he said
Life will put him down instead
Neither do I approve of his blood-sucking
Nor do I approve of your backbiting
[*Kolliyat*, p. 350]

In *Golestan* there is another story from personal experience con-
demning backbiting:

I remember that in childhood I was pious, rising for prayers during
the night, and eager for asceticism and abstinence. One night I was
sitting with my father – God's blessing be upon him – and was awake
all night holding the beloved Qor'an, while a group of people were
sleeping around us. I told my father 'Not one of these people rises
from bed to say a prayer. They are in such deep sleep as if they are
dead rather than asleep.' My father said 'My dear boy, if you too went
to sleep, it would be better than getting under the people's skin':

The claimant sees no one but himself
His eyes being covered by the veil of conceit
If they grant him the eye to see God
He will find no one weaker than himself
[*Kolliyat*, p. 74.]

There is in *Bustan* yet another story from childhood experience. He says that once as a boy he got the desire to fast. A pious neighbour taught him in great detail how to wash himself ritually before fasting, and pointed out that he must also wash his teeth as that was not permitted during the fasting period. When he had finished giving instructions he boasted that no one knew these rituals better than him, including the village headman who, he said, was old and redundant. The headman heard this remark and replied: "You said that washing one's teeth while fasting is not permitted. What made you think that eating the flesh of the dead [i.e. backbiting] is allowed?"

There then follow these verses on the subject in general:

When a person's name is mentioned
Speak of him in the best possible taste
When you keep saying everyone is an ass
Others will not call you a human being, alas!
Speak about me in public such that
In my own face you could say that
And if you are just ashamed of saying it
In my presence, is not God always present?
Are you not ashamed of yourself to be
Ashamed, not of the Almighty but of me?
[*Kolliyat*, pp. 351–352.]

The above story is followed by one about a group of dervishes. One of them began to backbite against an absent person. Another member of the group asked him if he had ever fought the Frankish in the Holy Land. He answered that he had never set foot out of his home. The other dervish expressed surprise that infidels were immune from him but Muslims were not:

My good man, when a friend is gone
Two things behind his back must not be done
One is to violate and waste his property
The other is to speak of him improperly
He who speaks badly of others
Do not expect good from his quarters
For he would say behind your back

The same as he has told you of others
He is correct and wise in this world
Who minds himself, not the world
[*Kolliyat*, p. 352]

Sa'di also teaches against informing someone of another person's negative comments about them, which can cause rift and animosity between the two: "Two people's fight is like a great fire/Its logs are supplied by the wretched informer":

Someone told a Sufi in Safa, do you know
What so-and-so said in your back about you?
He said, brother it is better to be asleep
Than to know what one's enemy speaks
He who takes my enemy's message to me
Is truly a bigger enemy than the enemy
No one would bring the word of one's enemy
Except he who is his partner in his enmity...
An informer helps renew an old fight again
For he provokes anger in a peaceful person
Try to avoid as much as possible
The companion who stirs up old trouble
He better be in a dungeon in shackles
Who brings trouble from place to place
Two people's fight is like a great fire
Its logs are supplied by the wretched informer
[*Kolliyat*, p. 353.]

Jealousy, as noted, is also condemned vehemently in Sa'di's works. Alongside with backbiting and malicious gossip, he describes it as one of the worst human habits and sentiments. Sa'di gives the clear impression that, not surprisingly, the poet himself had been a regular target of those who were jealous of his fame and success. In *Golestan* there is the story of a youthful courtier who was extremely bright and brilliant: "Above his head by his intelligence/Was shining the star of highness." The shah took a special interest in him despite his youth, "since he was beautiful both in appearance and in reality." And as wise men have observed: "Fortune arises from art, not wealth; and maturity is due to intelligence, not age":

His colleagues became jealous of him, accused him of treason, and uselessly made every effort towards his destruction: What can the enemy do when friend is kind? The shah asked him 'What is the cause of their enmity towards you?' He said, 'In your lordship's good fortune I made every one happy except those jealous of me who will not be happy but by the decline of my fortune and the lord's kindness towards me':

I can try not to hurt anyone except
The jealous person who hurts himself
Die o' jealous one, since this is a pain
For which except death all remedy is in vain
*
The unlucky wish and desire
That the lucky fall from power
If the moth's eye cannot see the day
It is not the fault of the sun's ray
A thousand eyes of that kind
Are better blind than the sun turned dark
[*Kolliyat*, p. 43.]

A similar story is told in a very long poem in chapter one of *Bustan*, "On Justice, Sound Government and Good Judgement." A wise and experienced stranger arrived in a land and quickly won the admiration of the shah. The shah decided to subject him to various tests over a period of time and, if he passed them, to make him his minister:

All of his manners and morals he tested
The man was God-fearing and intelligent
His morals were good, he was sound in logic
He knew every one's worth, his speech skilled
His judgement he found better than the notables
He placed him above his vizier, more valuable

The man conducted his office well. He employed such persuasive skills that he did not upset anyone when he gave out his orders. "He brought a whole realm under his pen" and yet no one had any cause to complain. The old vizier was jealous but could not find an excuse for campaigning against him, until he noticed the man's friendly relations with two of the shah's beautiful slaves. He accused him of being traitorous and a slave to his passion. The shah was indignant but, being a patient and deliberate ruler, he decided to try and discover the truth for himself. One day he caught the man and one of the pretty slaves exchanging a smile. He did not take hasty action but confronted the man and told him of the report of the old minister:

> Putting his hand on the mouth he smiled and said
> He was not surprised at the vizier's claim
> The jealous person who sees me occupy his place
> Could not be anything to me but a menace
> The minute he was put below my position
> I knew I would be prone to his sedition
> When the shah puts above him my standing
> No wonder that he turns into my enemy
> Not until doomsday will he be my friend
> For he sees my success as his own failure

The story goes on at some length, and the man explains that his years are far too advanced for any amorous adventures. His admiration of the young person's beauty is just like that of a poor man for the rich man's splendour. He simply admires what he had had in his youth and has since lost.

In the middle of the story there is an interesting digression on someone seeing in a dream the devil, tall and handsome. He asks the devil why he is totally unlike his popular image, as seen in pictures. The devil answers that this is because "the brush is in the enemy's hand":

> Where I read it, I do not recall
> That in a dream someone saw the devil
> Tall as cypress tree, pretty as gem
> Light shone from him like the sun
> He went forward and showed surprise
> Saying 'Not even angels are so nice
> Since you look like the moon shining
> Why do they think that you are disgusting?
> Why has the painter in the shah's court
> Painted you ugly, angry and spoilt?'
> When the poor devil thus heard him
> He cried loud, wept and told him

'O' happy man, I am not like that
But the brush is in the enemy's hand'
[*Kolliyat*, pp. 215–220.]

Finally, there is a story in chapter seven of *Bustan* in which, when
the actual tale ends, Sa'di spares a couple of verses in appreciation
of his own work:

Every line that I write is a mask
Holding under it a beautiful face
There is meaning beneath the black letter
Like clouded moon and veiled beloved
Dullness is not found in Sa'di's pages
Since they hide so many beauties
Words that enlighten the surroundings
Like fire, lighting up as well as burning
Should I be hurt when enemies dire?
They are feverish from this Persian fire!

Having penned these verses in appreciation of his own art and his
enemies' jealousy of it, he then launches into a long proclamation
about people's fault-finding about each other. It is a little masterpiece
in its own right: it is very well expressed, and it covers virtually the
whole range of human action and negative reaction. It begins with
verses saying that only those who shun society could be immune
from the jealousy and ill will of others. Whether a person is pious
or frivolous he cannot escape the injury afflicted by other people's
tongues:

Even if you fly up like an angel
The ill-wisher will not leave you alone
It may be possible to block Tigris River
But you cannot shut the mouth of an ill-wisher...
Do not think, whether you are a lion or fox
That you can escape the people's tongues
If a recluse sits by himself clean
That on others' company he is not keen
They would call him a two-faced hypocrite
Shunning people like a demon freed

But if he is friendly, then alas
They accuse him of being lax
They skin the rich man behind his back
That he is the pharaoh incarnate
But when a poor man complained
They would call him base and wretched
And if a successful man falls from favour
They rejoice and thank God with fervour
Saying 'How long can one be happy
After happiness you must be unhappy'
But if a man, poor and impecunious
Rises by good fortune to a higher status
They would bear him the poisonous grudge
That 'base people will have all the luck'
When they see you hard-working and honest
They call you greedy and materialist
And if you are not active and engaging
They will call you beggarly and sponging
If you speak well, you are an empty ball
If you are silent you are a picture on the wall
A tolerant person is not man enough
The wretched man is afraid of being tough
But if he has courage and manliness
They shun him saying this is madness
They find fault with he who eats frugally
'Destined for others is his property?'
But if he ate food full of taste and goodness
They would call him lazy and gluttonous...
If an ascetic does not travel around
They call him not a man, earth-bound:
'He who has not left his wife's embrace
Could not have any art, technique or grace'
But they likewise skin the traveller
That he is an unfortunate wanderer:
'If he was fortunate he would not
Be pushed from town to town'
The faultfinder blames the bachelor
That when he sleeps the earth shakes under

But if he marries, the faultfinder claims
That his whim threw him down on his head...
No one could escape the censure of others
The remedy is just patience and forbearance
[*Kolliyat*, pp. 360–362.]

6

THE WAYS OF SHAHS AND VIZIERS

S a'di, like virtually all the non-mystic classical Persian poets, was in contact with rulers and notables, although some mystic poets such as Hafiz also had relations with the court. In chapter 2 it was explained why he should not be described as a court poet, in spite of his contact with the court and courtiers, and also despite the fact that he did write a small number of eulogies. These eulogies often included admonitions and advice to the great to be just and fair in their treatment of their subjects.

Apart from the Solghorids (or Atabeigs) of Fars and their ministers and secretaries, he had other patrons, the two most important of whom were the Joveini brothers, great ministers of the Ilkhan emperor. According to a legend recorded in old manuscripts of his works he was once travelling in Tabriz and visited the Joveini brothers who proudly introduced him to the emperor Abaqa Khan as their "spiritual father."[53] According to another account, likewise recorded in old manuscripts, the elder Joveini, Shams al-Din, once wrote him a letter in which he asked him three questions and made one request.

The first question was: who were better, the Alavis (descendants of the prophet Mohammad through his daughter Fatima and son-in-law Ali), or non-Alavis? His answer was diplomatic. He wrote in a short poem that he had never seen an Alavi who drank alcohol and gambled. Therefore he was concerned lest at Resurrection the Prophet would be so busy interceding on their behalf that he would not have time to defend non-Alavis like them. Thus he does not say that they are better; merely that in his experience they did not commit two Islamic sins.

The next question was whether Hajjis or non-Hajjis were better. Here he makes a very scathing remark about Hajjis without answering the question directly:

> Tell the Hajji who hurts the people
> Him who viciously skins the people
> You are not a Hajji it is the camel
> Which carries burdens and eats thistle

The camel of course was used as the beast of burden by those who could afford it to cross the desert to Mecca. These verses are also written in a story in *Golestan*, but that is not unusual because Sa'di occasionally repeats some verses in different contexts.

The last question is on what Joveini should do with an enemy of his. The answer is typical of Sa'di's fair as well as realistic approach to such questions and of his style of versification in such subjects:

> First is advice and admonition
> Second is house arrest and prison
> Third is repentance and regret
> Fourth are oath and agreement
> Fifth behead the wicked man
> Who is begging for a bad fate

Finally, the minister made a request. He had asked the poet to accept a gift of 500 dinars (silver coins) which he had sent along with the letter. The amount of the money had not been mentioned in the letter out of courtesy, calling it a sum "for feeding the chickens." The courier going from Tabriz to Shiraz decided to include himself among the chickens and invest 150 dinars of the money in Isfahan, because Sa'di had previously turned down gifts of money. Sa'di sensed that the 350 dinars he received were short of the total amount sent, but accepted it and wrote the following verses in gratitude:

> My lord you sent me gift and money
> I pray for the growth of your money

And the downfall of your enemy
May for every dinar you live one year
So you live for three hundred and fifty years

When the courier took back Sa'di's reply to Shams al-Din, the vizier asked him what he had done with the money and he explained the reason for his action. Ala al-Din Ata Malek, Shams al-Din's brother and the other great vizier, was present. He wrote a letter of credit to a banker in Shiraz (whose name is mentioned in the text) instructing him to pay 10,000 dinars to Sa'di. When the letter reached Shiraz the banker was dead. Sa'di wrote back in verse thanking the vizier profusely, giving the news of the banker's death and saying that he would not claim the money from his estate, thus leaving it for his family. On reading the poet's reply the vizier ordered 50,000 drachmas (gold coins) to be sent to him, begging him to take the money and build a guesthouse with it in Shiraz for visitors to the city. Sa'di accepted and built the guesthouse, the name and location of which are mentioned in the text.[54]

The questions and answers look quite authentic, but the story of the gifts may have intermingled with legend, though there is no reason to doubt that Sa'di had received gifts of money from the Joveini brothers.

SHAHS

The first chapter of *Bustan*, "On Justice, Sound Government and Good Judgement," and the first chapter of *Golestan*, "On the Manners of Rulers," generally concern government, justice, the ways and manners of shahs and the difficult role of ministers and other notables. The chapter in *Bustan* is somewhat more abstract and didactive than that in *Golestan*, which is more about real-life experiences. But stories and admonitions regarding rulers and ministers are not confined only to these two chapters and may be found elsewhere in both books.

It was noted in chapter 2 that neither these two books, nor even their more specialized chapters mentioned above, may be realistically described as "mirrors for princes." Nor are they about "politics" although

they *are* about *siyasat*, meaning both the art of managing a realm successfully and the punishment, fairly or unfairly, of viziers, notables and
others in the service of or connected to the court and state.

There was no law in the sense of a long-enduring and inviolable
body of rules or traditions to which the ruler was also bound. Law
was the will and whim of the ruler which could change by a clap of
the hands. Judicial or *shari'a* law was applicable only when it did not
clash with the will of the state. As there was no law, in the generally accepted sense as described above, neither was there politics,
or it was not much different from the "politics" within a traditional
household when its various members strive for higher benefits and
lower costs within the changeable rules set by the arbitrary patriarch.
When reading Sa'di, as well as the other Persian classics, we must
bear in mind that government in those times was always arbitrary
and often also absolute; furthermore, since it was arbitrary, it was
different even from the despotic governments which ruled Europe
between the sixteenth and twentieth centuries.

Thus arbitrary government was taken for granted as being natural,
in the sense that no one believed that there could be another system
of government and that therefore no one described and advocated an
alternative to it. It was not until the nineteenth century that models
of European government showed that arbitrary rule was not the
only form of government, and hence reforming intellectuals began
to discuss and campaign for government based in law. Before then,
and throughout ancient as well as classical periods, all government
was assumed to be arbitrary and hence the question of good government was centred on whether or not the government was just. Given
the nature of personal rule, justice depended almost entirely on the
character and attitude of the ruler.[55]

Sa'di describes and criticizes the rulers and advises them to be
just, fair, patient in taking decisions, especially when they affect
other people's lives and fortunes, and do what they can to protect
their realms, including acts and attitudes which will meet with the
approval of their subjects. The advocacy of justice is in the Persian
classical sense, i.e., equal treatment of subjects and servants, and
the establishment of peace and stability which will result in material

improvement as well as freedom from chaos. Unlike the authors of "mirrors for princes" he does not advise rulers merely on how to gain power and/or maintain and enhance it. Rather, through stories, tales, anecdotes, parables, aphorisms and metaphors, he charges the rulers to behave such that their subjects will be content and they themselves will not be ashamed when they meet their Maker in the next world. He often threatens them both with the curse and revolt of the people and with punishment at Resurrection.

Unlike some other writers and thinkers, before and since, Sa'di does not regard government as such as being illegitimate, nor does he think that an ascetic or dervish is necessarily better than a ruler. In other words, as noted in chapter 2 in the debate on the rich and poor, he does not judge the people by their social class and category but by their personal attitude and behaviour. A ruler may be good and just and a dervish bad and unjust, as well as the other way round. This he makes most clear in a story in *Bustan* in which a ruler thinks of giving up his throne and becoming a dervish. But when he consults a wise and just man he is told: "You remain on your royal throne/But be a dervish by good deeds and tone":

It is in the traditions of former shahs
That when Tokleh mounted the throne
In his time he did not hurt anyone
Thus it was that he superseded everyone
One day he told a man, wise and just
That my life has gone to waste as such
I would like to sit in a corner and pray
To live usefully now until Judgement's Day...
When the enlightened man heard all that
He reacted harshly and said 'Tokleh stop!
Serving God is nothing but serving the folks
Not the rosary the prayer-mat and ragged clothes
You remain on your royal throne
But be a dervish by good deeds and tone'
[*Kolliyat*, p. 225.]

The very first story with which *Golestan* begins is interesting in various ways, including the fact that it was used out of context by Sa'di's

Iranian detractors of the second half of the twentieth century (briefly discussed in chapter 1) to claim that he had advocated lying:

I was told that a shah ordered the execution of a captive. In that hopeless state the unfortunate man began to curse the shah and swear at him: He who forfeits his life would say whatever is in his heart:

In dire trouble with no escape in sight
One would resort to the sword and fight
*
When one loses hope he loosens his tongue
Like the cornered cat which assaults the dog

The shah asked what he was saying. A well-meaning minister said 'Lord, he says "Those who overcome their anger and forgive [are beneficent]."' [The sentence in quotation marks is a direct quotation in Arabic from the Qor'an.]

The shah was moved with compassion and stopped his execution. The other minister who was contrary to the first one said that 'people of our kind should not speak but the truth in the presence of shahs. This man swore at the shah and cursed him.' The shah frowned upon hearing this and said; 'I like his falsehood better than the truth which you uttered, since that was based on expediency, and this, on wickedness. And they have said that "an expedient lie is better than a seditious truth."'

He whose advice the shah accepts
Pity if he says but pleasant things

On the ceiling of the portal of Fereydun's palace it was written:

The world, my brother, will not last to anyone
Try to love the world Creator and no other one
Do not depend on the kingdom of this world
For many like you it raised and destroyed
*
When the pure soul sets out from this world
It is equal, dying on the throne or on the floor
[*Kolliyat*, pp. 37–38.]

Thus it is clear that, contrary to his detractors, Sa'di has not advocated lying. He simply says that the shah thought that the good-

natured minister's attempt to save the prisoner's life was commend-
able. And this is not inconsistent even with modern ethics. It is also
important to note that the entire event takes place in the context of
the arbitrary exercise of power. In the same way that the shah had
decided to have the man executed he decided to set him free by a
change of mood. Throughout Iranian history courtiers and notables
intervened from time to time to save the life of those who had fallen
victim to the wrath or hasty decisions of rulers, for in that situation
there was no legal procedure that could come to their aid.

A similar theme occurs in a short anecdote in the same chapter of
the same book. A shah ordered an innocent man to be executed. The
man told him not to bring harm to himself just out of anger towards
him. He explained that his own execution would only take a minute,
whereas its guilt would be carried by the shah for ever:

> The cycle of life moved like wind in the desert
> Joy and bitterness, beauty and ugliness passed away
> The unjust person thought he was unkind to us
> It passed us by but remained on his head anyway
> [*Kolliyat*, pp. 63–64.]

THE TRANSIENCE OF POWER AND EXISTENCE

The transience of life and its joys is one of the points Sa'di emphasizes most, to the mighty in particular, although not exclusively, as
a reminder that life is not worth the arrogance of power and possessions and the injustice of inflicting pain on the less fortunate. The
following tale is a masterpiece both for its content and for the way
it has been expressed, including its brevity, which is characteristic
of Sa'di's prose as well as poetry:

> A ruler of Khorasan saw Mahmud son of Saboktegin in his dream
> such that the whole of his body had been depleted and turned into
> dust except his eyes that were still turning in their sockets. None of
> the learned men could interpret that dream except a dervish who
> said: He still looks and wonders that his realm is owned by others:

Many a great one they have buried under the earth
Of whose existence no sign remained on the earth
And when they committed that old corpse to dust
Dust eroded it and no bone remained in sight
Do good o' so-and-so and enjoy this life before
A voice is heard that so-and-so remains no more
[*Kolliyat*, p. 38.]

Generally along the same lines is the following short anecdote:

Someone took Anushiravan the Just the good news that 'God removed
such-and-such enemy of yours from this world here'. He said 'Did
you think that he would let me remain for ever?'

Do not rejoice in the death of an enemy
We too will pass away on another day
[*Kolliyat*, p. 67.]

Once again on the transience of power and existence there is the
story in *Golestan* of a dying Arab ruler:

An Arab ruler was old and unwell and had given up hope of living
when a rider arrived and delivered the good news that 'we conquered
such-and-such a castle and captured the enemies, and its soldiers and
civilians have all been subjected'. The ruler heaved a cold sigh and
said that this is not good news for me but for my enemies, i.e. those
who will inherit the realm:

My dear life was spent alas in the hope
That what I desire will arrive at my door
The hope was fulfilled but it is hopeless because
There is no hope that spent-life will return once more
*
Death is beating the drum for departure
O' my two eyes say farewell to my head
O' my palm, my wrist, my arm
Say farewell to one another calm
Friends please see me off, right
Now that I am down to my enemies' delight
In ignorance did I pass my life
You try not to regret your life
[*Kolliyat*, p. 46.]

IDEAL GOVERNMENT

The preamble to chapter one of *Bustan*, "On Justice, Sound Government and Good Judgement," contains a virtually comprehensive list of instructions for ideal government. They are attributed to Anushiravan the Just speaking to his son Hormoz on his death bed:

> At the point of death, so I have heard
> Anushiravan talked to Hormoz and said
> Try to look after the poor and needy
> Do not only think of your well-being
> No one will live in peace and comfort
> If you seek only your own betterment
> No wise man would approve of the shepherd
> Who sleeps and lets the wolf among the herd...
> The sultan is a tree, his subjects are the roots
> The tree stands on the strength of its roots
> Do what you can not to hurt the people's feeling
> And if you do, your own roots you are peeling...
> Only in his dream would he see the land flourish
> Whose people he would ruin and impoverish...
> Whatever you decide on make sure
> That the subjects' good it would ensure...
> Subjects will run away from an unjust ruler
> And would give him a bad name the world over...
> A soldier cannot cause as much harm
> As women and children cursing from their heart...
> Since both good and bad work pass eventually
> Better to leave a good name behind permanently
> [*Kolliyat*, pp. 211–212.]

In *Golestan* there are several tales and stories regarding the question of justice by rulers towards their subjects. Sometimes Anushiravan or some other shahs from antiquity are used as models for justice and good government. Occasionally Harun al-Rashid and his son Ma'mun, the great Abbasid caliphs, are cited as examples. Sometimes fictitious rulers are used to denounce injustice and show its dire consequences in this and the next world. In one tale, Anushiravan is made to say that

if the shah violates the subjects' property and possessions his soldiers
and servants will do the same, only much more severely:

> It has been said that in a hunting ground they were roasting game for
> Anushiravan but did not have salt. One of his guards went to the nearby
> village to bring salt. Anushiravan told him 'Buy the salt at market price
> so that a bad tradition is not started which would result in the ruin of the
> village.' The guard said 'What damage will come of such a small thing?'
> He answered: 'The foundation of injustice in the world was at first very
> small. Each person added something to it until it became so big':

> If the shah eats one apple from his subject's orchard
> His guards will pull out the tree by the root
> When the sultan allows injustice for five eggs
> His soldiers will take a thousand chickens to roast
> [*Kolliyat*, pp. 55–56.]

In contrast to this is the story of the unjust governor who bought
the woodcutters' logs cheap and sold it in the market at a high
price. Here Sa'di uses the term *tarh* which was a non-canonical tax
exacted by the government acting as a monopolistic buyer, buying
the producers' goods at an arbitrarily low price and selling them in
the market at a high price, and so exacting the "tax" as the difference
between the purchase and sale prices. Thus he is attacking what was
usually common practice in the government's fiscal policy:

> They say that an unjust governor used to buy the woodcutters' log
> very cheaply and sell it to the well-to-do as *tarh*. An enlightened man
> once saw him and said:

> You are a snake who bites everyone it sees
> Or a bird of bad omen which ruins wherever it sits
> *
> If you use force against us
> You cannot use it against God
> Do not use force against the people
> So they do not curse you before God

> The governor was hurt and paid no attention either to him or to
> his advice. One night the fire in his kitchen fell into his wood store
> and all of his properties burnt down and he was brought from his

comfortable bed down to a carpet of warm ashes. By chance the same man passed him by and heard him say to his friends 'I do not know whence this fire fell into my residence.' He told him 'It came from the heart of the poor'

> It was written on the crown of Key Khosraw:
> Many years and ages will pass that
> People will walk over our heads
> We received the kingdom
> From one hand to the next
> It will pass to other hands as well
> *Kolliyat*, pp. 60–61.

In a short and brilliant anecdote in *Golestan* an unjust ruler asks an ascetic which mode of worshipping God is best. The ascetic answers: "For you it is mid-day sleep so for one moment you will not hurt the people":

> I saw an unjust ruler sleeping at mid-day
> I said he is trouble, he better be asleep
> And he who is better asleep than awake
> Would be better dead than alive
> [*Kolliyat*, pp. 47–48.]

In both books justice is advocated in a very wide sense of the term which includes generosity, kindness, tolerance and forgiveness. Rulers must promote welfare, look after their soldiery, overcome their anger, not execute anyone at the first offence, and show patience and forbearance in dealing with offenders. The following verses in *Bustan* instruct the ruler to show patience and not easily resort to the execution of a suspected offender:

> Forgive the guilty when they repent
> When they ask for mercy, grant them
> If a guilty person begs for forgiveness
> Do not kill him at the first offence
> If he was advised and did not listen
> Punish him by putting him in prison
> If neither advice nor prison was heeded
> Then as a rotten tree he should be uprooted

When someone's guilt provokes your anger
Put him not to death but hold your temper
For it is easy to break the ruby of Badakhshan
But impossible to put the pieces together again
[*Kolliyat*, pp. 214–215.]

On the same theme, and especially of hesitation on ordering capital punishment, he says again in the same book, this time specifically addressing the contemporary ruler of Fars:

Jail the guilty person before killing
For you cannot bring him back to living...
A proud head, empty of patience
The royal crown it does not deserve
He who is rational and wise will put up
If his reason holds, as anger turns up
When anger assaults like an army
There will be no fairness, faith or piety
[*Kolliyat*, p. 220.]

In *Golestan* he advises the ruler to tolerate insults to himself through a story he relates from Harun al-Rashid:

A son of Harun al-Rashid came to see his father and said that 'the son of such-and-such officer has called my mother a bad name'. Harun asked his advisers what the punishment of such a person should be. One of them suggested execution, another the mutilation of his tongue, yet another confiscation of his property and expulsion from town. Harun told his son 'It would be magnanimous to forgive, but if you cannot forgive, you too call his mother a bad name, so that retribution will not go beyond the offence, for in that case we would be the unjust and the enemy, the aggrieved party':

A wise man will not think as gallant
A person who fights a mighty elephant
The person is brave who at point of anger
Will not loosen his tongue in rancour
[*Kolliyat*, pp. 65–66.]

OTHER-WORLDLINESS

In a story in *Bustan* Sa'di brings up the question of the transience of life in this world once again, this time in connection with a ruler's loss of temper and the resulting unjust punishment of an innocent man. But here more than elsewhere is evident the spirit of other-worldliness which runs through many if not most of his writings on justice and morality. He says that a ruler unjustly imprisoned a man and when he was not cowed by his punishment he ordered the mutilation of his tongue. But he still remained serene saying that he would be blessed in the other world:

> I have heard that once a mighty ruler
> Was offended by a humble courtier
> Having expressed a just view on a matter
> His frankness had angered the ruler
> He sent the man to jail from the court
> To the use of force would power resort
> A friend told the prisoner in secret
> 'What you did was not expedient'
> He said 'God's command must be told
> Jail for no more than a moment will hold'
> He had expressed himself thus no sooner
> Than the shah heard it from an informer
> He laughed and said 'He is mistaken
> He knows not that he will die in prison'

The emphasis on the virtues of other-worldliness comes at this point:

> A guard took this message to the man
> Who told the guard 'Tell the shah for me
> I am not sad and my heart is not hurt
> For this world is no more than a moment
> Neither would I rejoice by your being kind
> Nor if you killed me would I mind
> When we enter the valley of death
> You and I will be equal within a breath
> Do not be attached to this world transient

Thus burning by the fire in the people's hearts...
Live such that they would admire you
When you died, not curse and damn you...'
These words angered the shah who ordered
The poor man's tongue to be mutilated
The enlightened man hearing, said
'Even of this I will have no dread...
What injustice or deprivation I may suffer
I will not mind for my end will be better'
[*Kolliyat*, pp. 244–245.]

Elsewhere in *Bustan* the poet makes the same point not through a story but directly as advice and admonishment to rulers. Here he openly threatens unjust rulers by the punishment that they will receive from the hand of Providence in this as well as the next world:

You have heard that some ancient shahs of Persia
Ruled with injustice the people of Persia
Neither did their majesty and pageantry last long
Nor did their injustice to the peasantry survive long
When an unjust ruler commits an injustice
The world survives but he dies with his injustice
Happy be in the Day of Judgement the just ruler
Who will be housed in the shadow of the Creator...
Know that your greatness is due to God's grace
For His blessings will not last with ungratefulness
The ruler does not deserve to sleep well
When under him the strong exploit the weak
Do not hurt the subjects as much as a pock
The sultan is the shepherd and subjects the flock
When they see harshness and injustice from him
He is not a shepherd but a wolf, woe to him
He who towards his subjects unjustly behaved
Would be cursed in this and the other world
If you do not wish to be damned behind your back
Be beneficent so no one will curse and attack
[*Kolliyat*, p. 230.]

In the same book there is a story from Omar ibn Abd al-Aziz, the pious Umayyad caliph who ruled a very large and prosperous empire. Once there was famine, presumably in Syria, since his seat was in Damascus. He sold the unique stone in his ring to pay for famine relief:

A great man of distinction and verity
Has told of the Son of Abd al-Aziz this story
That in his ring he had a stone, such wonder
No price could be set on it by the jeweller
It glittered at night with such light
Like a gate that opened the day to night
Since he saw the people in dire misery
He thought it unfair for him to be happy
When one sees poison in the people's mouth
How can he let pleasant water down his throat?
He ordered the stone to be sold for money
For on orphans and strangers he took pity
Within a week he gave the cash away
To dervishes, the poor and the needy

And when they told him he would never find the like of that stone:

They say he spoke while a torrent of tears
Like a candle was running down his face
Luxury is wrong for a ruler to enjoy
When a city is miserable, without joy
I could live with a ring that has no stone
But of suffering a people should not moan
He is blessed who puts the comfort
Of men and women above his own
[Kolliyat, p. 224.]

In contrast to that is the long story of the ruler who took the people's asses by force. Once he became lost while travelling and had to spend the night incognito in a village. There he overheard a farmer tell his son not to take his ass to town next morning because the unjust ruler would take it from him. And as he spoke he was vehemently cursing and abusing the ruler. Next morning the ruler's guards found him in the village.

He sent them to bring the old man and ordered him to be executed. The old man told him that he was not the only person who thought so ill of him: "I told you in the front/others say it at the back":

> When you rule unjustly do not expect
> Your name to be mentioned with respect...
> In stopping injustice is your redemption
> Not in killing a poor innocent person ...
> The unjust person will not for ever reign
> But lasting damnation of him will remain
> [*Kolliyat*, pp. 239–243.]

There are a few stories about the attitude of pious subjects towards shahs and rulers. In chapter 4 the story was mentioned of the shah who regarded a group of dervishes with contempt. One of them said: "O ruler, we are less than you in arms in this world present, but our life is more pleasant; at death we are your equal and will be better than you at Resurrection." Also in *Golestan* is the story of the dervish who offended a shah by ignoring him:

> A reclusive dervish was living in an isolated spot. A shah passed
> him by but, given the lack of need associated with the realm of
> contentment, the dervish did not acknowledge him. Given the
> majesty of kingship, the sultan was hurt and said 'These ascetics are
> like animals and lack civility and humanity.' The vizier approached
> the dervish and said 'Chivalrous sir, the lord of the land passed you
> by. Why did you not display humbleness and show respect to him?'
> He replied 'Tell the sultan to expect service from one who expects
> a favour from him. And further than that, he should know that shahs
> exist for protecting the subjects, not the subjects for serving shahs':

> The shah is the protector of the subjects
> Though his majestic reign results in peace
> The sheep does not exist for the shepherd
> It is the shepherd that must serve the sheep...

> The shah understood and accepted the view of the dervish. He said
> 'Ask a favour from me'. The dervish replied 'Please do not bother me
> again'. The shah said, 'Give me a piece of advice'. He replied:

Be careful now that the reins are in your hand
For the reins of power pass from hand to hand
[*Kolliyat*, pp. 62–63.]

But the man in *Bustan* who likewise did not show respect to the cruel
Hajjaj ibn Yusuf was not so lucky:

They say about a good man who
Respect to Hajjaj he did not show
Hajjaj told the officer at the court
To seat him down and cut his throat
The man of God first smiled then cried
At this the cruel ruler was surprised
When he saw him first smile then cry
He asked the cause of cry and smile
He said "I cry because in this world
I have little children four in all
I smile because by God's kindness
I shall not die guilty of injustice
The son of Hajjaj said 'Show mercy
And spare the life of this Sufi…
Show greatness and be magnanimous
Think of his little children's happiness'
He did not listen and had him killed
(From one's fate no-one is freed)
That night a good man mindful of this
Dreamed of the Sufi and asked about him
'It took him a moment' he said 'to kill me
Till the Resurrection he will suffer for it'
[*Kolliyat*, p. 234.]

There is also advice in both books that rulers should not unfairly
destroy the reputation of their predecessors. In *Golestan* he relates a
tradition from Alexander:

They asked Alexander the Greek 'How did you manage to conquer
the West as well as East, since the former rulers were older and
richer and had bigger armies than you.' He said 'By the grace of God
any kingdom that I conquered I did not harm the people and did not
mention the [previous] rulers' names except with respect':

Wise men will not call him great
Who respects not the names of the great
[*Kolliyat*, p. 69.]

In *Bustan* there is direct advice – apparently to the contemporary
ruler – in the following verses:

If you wish your name for ever to remain
Do not spoil the good name of the great
The same picture remains after your time
That you now see after the past shahs
They too had the same joy and pleasure
But left, and left behind their treasure
Someone leaves a good name in the world
Another leaves a bad tradition to behold
[*Kolliyat*, p. 214.]

The above account was a discussion of Sa'di's writings on shahs and
rulers in *Golestan* and *Bustan*. He also has a little book or long essay
that consists solely of 151 counsels addressed to rulers. Although
this has been published in his collected works it is virtually unknown
and is seldom if ever cited. It bears exactly the same title as Ghazali's
bigger *Nasihat al-Moluk* or Counsels for Rulers and is likely to have
been so named with that book in mind. Most of these counsels are
the same or similar to those which have been put forward in *Bustan*
and *Golestan*, but here they are offered directly in short statements.
He says in its preamble that "a dear friend" had asked him to write
the booklet. The counsels almost equally relate to the means of success for rulers in this as well as the other world. It could be fairly
claimed that, in terms of the thirteenth century there is hardly any
point regarding justice, fairness, good government, prosperity, peace
and security that is not covered in it:

Of the ways of rulers one is that at night they beg at God's threshold
and during the day rule over the people.

As will be seen from the following sample, putting aside the purely
moral counsels they are based on realism not idealism, and therefore
there is an emphasis on moderation:

Magnanimity is good but not to the point of the government getting weak and facing hardship; and economizing is expedient but not such that the soldiery and others go without.

And so it is regarding judgment and punishment:

They saw Anushiravan the Just, who was an Infidel, in a dream living in beautiful surroundings. They asked him 'How did you manage to find such an exalted place?' He said 'I did not pity the criminals and did not hurt the innocent'.

The shah should not engage a strong enemy since it is against his interest, and should not bully the meek because it is unfair:

One of the conditions of good government by a shah is that he would not fight a strong enemy and would not hurt the weak, because to fight a dominant power is inexpedient and to twist the hands of the weak, contrary to fairness.

He ends the counsels by advising the shah to listen to his own advice, and this indicates his status and influence at the time:

The shah should honestly and sincerely listen to these counsels of Sa'di so that, with the help of God, his realm and faith would be safe, himself and his children would be well [and] this world and the next would be according to his wishes...
[*Kolliyat*, pp. 871–887.]

VIZIERS

Sa'di says in *Golestan* "A companion of the sultan may one day receive gold and another day lose his head."[56] This sums up the situation of viziers and courtiers in the system of arbitrary government. The main difference between this system and Europe was that anyone with any class and social background could become vizier, the second most powerful man in the realm, more powerful even than princes of the blood. But by the same logic and sociology any vizier, however able and powerful, could lose his head at a clap of the ruler's hands, sometimes together with his family, his clan and his possessions.

There were two inter-related differences from normal European traditions when it came to punishing viziers and notables. First, mere anger based on suspicion was sufficient for their destruction and, secondly, there would be no recourse to any court of law or independent hearing once their fate was determined by the ruler. Punishment was usually horrific. Besides, as noted, their families and clan could be likewise destroyed, and whatever they possessed was bound to be confiscated: "They do not heed the end of the vizier/ Who for nine years hung from the gallows."

Given the meritocratic nature 'of the process whereby ministers and other high officials were selected, they were usually able and intelligent men. Consequently, the abler they were the more powerful they became, which ironically put them in greater danger of fall and destruction. Of the viziers who were disgraced, banished or, as was more common, executed the following were some of the greatest of the shahs, from the tenth to the twentieth century: Abolfazl Bala'mi, Abolfath Bosti, Abol'abbas Esferayeni, Ahmad son of Hasan Meimandi, Hasanak the Vizier, Amid al-Molk Kondori, Nezam al-Molk Tusi, Ahmad Zia' al-Molk, Shams al-Din Joveini, Rashid al-Din Fazlollah, Emamqoli Khan, Hajj Ebrhim Kalantar, Qa'em-Maqam, Amir Kabir, Aqa Khan Nuri, Teymurtash, Sardar As'ad and Nosrat al-Dawleh (Firuz).

Vizier-killing and regicide were also part of the pre-Islamic Persian culture and have been documented in *Shahnameh* as well as Greek and Roman sources. According to Ferdowsi's *Shahnameh*, when Hormoz succeeded his father Anushiravan he ordered the execution of all of his father's ministers and counsellors. Sa'di says he imprisoned them, and his explanation is that because they feared him, he too was afraid of them:

They asked Hormoz what fault you found with your father's ministers which made you put them in jail. He said 'I did not see any fault in them. But I realized that the fear of me was boundless in them and they did not trust my pledge for their safety. I was afraid that because of their fear of me they might decide to kill me'
[*Kolliyat*, p. 45.]

This dialectic of fear was in fact the most basic cause of both vizier-killing and regicide, which arose from treachery, greed or mere suspicion and paranoia. In the nineteenth century, Naser al-Din Shah was about to blind his thirteen-year-old brother on the mere suspicion that some unknown persons might conspire to bring him down and put his brother on the throne. The British and Russian envoys intervened and eventually saved the boy. Before that happened, the logic of such injustice was explained by the vizier to the British envoy when he said justice in Iran made it necessary to take action on the slightest suspicion and supposition. The logic was that if one side did not move quickly enough the other side might move more quickly. This arose mainly from the fact that in the system of arbitrary rule, there was no primogeniture, i.e. anyone other than the first son of the shah could replace him if he managed to seize the throne.[57]

Furthermore, it was not just the shah who ruled arbitrarily but anyone, minister, governor or other high official, who ruled in his name also took arbitrary decisions within his domain so long as they did not contradict directly the wishes of the shah or the official immediately above them. That is how ministers and notables could also commit arbitrary injustice and why they were usually unpopular among the people. Sa'di says in the last chapter of *Golestan*:

> What could an old whore do but repent from wickedness; and a
> fallen police chief, from hurting the people?
> [*Kolliyat*, p. 192.]

This is the background and the framework in which Sa'di's stories and comments on the relationship of shahs and viziers and of viziers with the people may be understood.

There is a story in *Golestan* that reflects many aspects of the insecurity of the life and property of viziers.

> A minister was dismissed and joined a group of dervishes. And their
> serenity made him calm and collected. Later the shah took a good
> view of him again and offered him a post. He did not accept and said
> 'To wise people being jobless is better than being involved':
>
> Those who sat in the corner of sound life
> Shut the dog's teeth and the people's mouth

> They broke the pen and tore off the papers
> And escaped the tongue of trouble-makers

The shah told him that he would need a wise man to run the country. He answered that the sign of a wise man is that he would not accept public office:

> The Homa is superior to all other birds
> Because it does not hurt anyone and eats bones

There follows a story within the story:

> They asked the caracal how he became a vassal of the lion. He said 'So that I feed from his hunt and live in his protection from my enemies.' They said 'Now that you are protected by him and confess to his beneficence why do you not get closer so he would make you a close companion?' He said 'Still I am not immune from his violence.'

And here comes the brilliant verse:

> If a Zoroastrian makes fire a hundred years
> The moment he falls in it he burns

> A companion of the sultan may one day receive gold and another day lose his head. And philosophers have said that one must be wary of the changing nature of the shahs' attitudes since sometimes they are offended by a greeting and at other times they will give a reward for a curse...
> [*Kolliyat*, p. 50.]

There is realism in the story about Anushiravan and his legendary vizier Bozorgmehr, who, however, spent much time in prison:

> Ministers of Anushiravan were pondering on an important matter regarding the interest of the state, and so was the shah himself. Bozorgmehr liked the shah's opinion. The ministers told him in confidence what advantage did you think the shah's opinion had over that of so many wise and experienced men. He said 'Because the consequences are not predictable, and everybody's opinion may turn out to be right or wrong. Therefore it is best to agree with the shah's view so that if it proves to be wrong, having followed him we would be immune from being castigated.'

To offer an opinion contrary to the sultan's
Is to wash one's hand in one's own blood
If he calls day night, one should exclaim:
'Look, the Pleiades and the moon!'
[*Kolliyat*, p. 62.]

This is clearly not advice to ministers to be hypocritical, or even
faithless, but it is to point out the real risk of contradicting the ruler's
views, and more generally to show the tenuous and precarious nature
of government service in an arbitrary system. In another, long story
Sa'di describes the rise, fall and recovery of a courtier, but what is
even more significant than the account of events is the conversation
between the narrator and the man:

One of my friends came to see me and complained that his income
was low, he had a large family and he could not bear his poverty. 'I
have thought of going somewhere else so that no matter how I live at
least no one would know about it:

So many slept hungry and no one noticed
So many people died and no one cried

But at the same time I am mindful of enemies who would laugh
behind my back and describe as unkind my leaving my family ... I
have no knowledge of accounting, but if by your influence I get a post
that would bring me ease of mind I would never be able to thank you
enough for it'. I said 'Brother, the sultan's service has two sides to it:
hope of provisions and fear of life. And it is contrary to the opinion of
the wise to embrace this fear for that hope:

The poor man's home no one will visit
To ask for the taxes of land and garden
Either put up with worry and sigh
Or expose your liver to the magpie'

He said 'This is not relevant to my case and does not address my
request. Have you not heard that "he who commits treason would
fear exposure with reason":

Honesty is approved by God
No one is lost in a straight path

And according to wise men four persons will have fear of four
persons: highwayman, of sultan; thief, of civil police; adulterer, of
informer; and prostitute of religious police. But he whose account is
clear, of auditors will not fear...'

At this point the allegorical tale of the fox and the camel is told which
says much about the hazards of public life in Iran. Different versions
of this tale had been told before, notably by Ragheb-e Isfahani and
Anvari Abivardi, but Sa'di's is the best and most amusing:

I said the story of that fox is relevant to your case that was seen fast
on the run and falling up and down. Someone asked it 'What is the
calamity that has caused such anxiety?' It said 'I have heard that they
are catching camels'. Someone said 'You idiot, what is the relevance of
the camel to you and you to it?' 'Silence,' it said. 'If those jealous of me
wickedly said that I am a camel, who would care to look at my situation
and try to save me, and by the time they bring the antidote from Iraq
snake bite will have killed the bitten person.' You have virtue, faith,
integrity and honesty. But malicious people are lying in wait and the
aspirants are gathered in a corner. If they speak about you contrary to
the good person you are, and the shah's anger turns on you, who would
be able to defend you? Therefore I think it is in your interest to keep to
the world of contentment and forget about becoming important:

In the sea lots of good things are galore
But if you want safety it is on the shore

Sa'di's friend was upset at this advice and felt that he did not wish
to help him: "Friends are useful when one is in prison; at the dinner
spread enemies look like friends":

He is not a friend who in good times
Bluffs about friendship and brotherliness
Friend is he who takes the friend's hand
When he is down and in distress

Having seen his anger he decided to help. He went and saw the
Sahab-divan or minister. This was the title of both of the aforemen-
tioned Jovieni brothers, and if the story has any basis in truth it
would therefore have happened in Tabriz. They gave his friend a

junior post but after a while, having seen his good nature and management ability they raised his status until he became a companion
of the sultan:

> At that time I went on a journey and when I returned from the
> pilgrimage of Mecca he came two leagues to welcome me. I found
> him distressed and looking like dervishes and asked him what had
> happened. He replied 'As you had anticipated some people became
> jealous of me and accused me of treason, and the shah – may his reign
> last – did not try to discover the truth, and old favourites and good
> friends did not tell the truth and forgot the old friendship':

> Do you not see how they bow
> To one with status and power
> But if fate brings him down
> All of them push him under?

> 'Anyhow I was subjected to all forms of punishment until this week
> the good news of safe return of the pilgrims arrived and they released
> me from jail and returned my hereditary estate to me.' I said 'Last
> time you did not accept my view that being an official of shahs is like
> going on a voyage, dangerous as well as profitable; either you will
> have a treasure or you will die without pleasure':

> You did not know that you will be in fetters
> When you do not listen to the advice of others
> Next time because you cannot bear sting
> Push not your finger into a scorpion's breach
> [Kolliyat, pp. 51–54.]

Finally, Sa'di's view about enjoying and suffering public office seems
to have been summed up in this little story:

> Two brothers, one of them was in the sultan's service, the other
> earned his living by his own effort. The rich brother told the common
> other 'Why do you not get into public service so you would be
> relieved of hard work?' He replied 'Why do you not work so you
> would be relieved of the degradation of service, since wise men have
> said that to eat one's bread independently is better than to wear a
> golden sword in service:

Better beat molten iron with one's hand
Than stand to the sultan with crossed hands'
[*Kolliyat*, pp. 66–67.]

Arbitrary rule in Iran was regarded as the natural system of government until the nineteenth century when the Iranian elite discovered
the system of government based in law through their observations
of European society. Before this, the alternative to arbitrary rule
was chaos. That is why men like Sa'di advised the rulers and their
ministers to be just and patient in using their power, and warned the
government officials that they were constantly in danger of falling
victim to the whims of the arbitrary rulers.

CONCLUDING REMARKS

Sa'di was an eclectic in the best sense of that term. He was familiar with most of the literary and intellectual frameworks of his time but unlike most thinkers and literati he did not work solely within any of them and so cannot be located in any given framework. He cannot be described as a rationalist, although he set a high store by reason and intellect and regarded intellectual knowledge as a necessary if not sufficient means for human advancement. Nor can he be called a mystic, despite the fact that he was closely familiar with the theory and practice of Sufism and admired the legendary grand Sufis. Philosophical realism – something akin to Socratic wisdom – is perhaps the nearest modern term that may be applied to his approach to personal and social life, although he was far from a pragmatist and instrumentalist.

Judging by his works, he was a savant, a *hakim*, who advocated tolerance, moderation and good sense. He did not believe in any conception of perfect life, only in a good, clean life, and for that reason he had a relatively optimistic outlook to life and was not too censorious of his fellow human beings. He did not promise, advocate, pray for or demand the establishment of heaven on earth, nor did he think that an imperfect world was not worth living in. He advocated striving for betterment, not longing for perfection. It is only in such broad terms that he may be compared with the Christian humanists of the Renaissance period such as Erasmus of Rotterdam. However, much caution must be used when making such comparisons between cultures of different times and places.

Yet Sa'di was not just a savant but more importantly a poet and writer. Indeed, our interest in him is mainly on that account, precisely as Rumi would not have attained his exceptionally high status among Islamic mystics if he had not at the same time been a poet, expressing his mystic love in his *ghazals* and his mystical ideas in his *mathnavi*. The impact of Sa'di's *Golestan* in Iran and Europe would not have been as great if its basic ideas were simply put together in a few pages of plain prose. The same is true of his *Bustan*, except that, being a poem, it loses much when translated into other tongues, and that must be an important reason why *Golestan* has enjoyed much greater popularity outside Iran. It has, however, had a wider appeal in Iran as well partly because it is a more amusing and less demanding book, and partly because it combines fact and fiction, parable and wisdom, admiration and admonition with the wittiest, simplest and clearest forms of expression. Once again, allowing for all the cultural, temporal and spatial differences, he reminds the reader – in this respect – of European writers such as Montaigne, Voltaire and Samuel Johnson, all of whom flourished long after he had gone.

It is difficult to compare *Golestan* with any of the "mirrors for princes" or "books of government" such as those written before it by Keikavus ibn Eskandar and Nezam al-Molk, as has been suggested by some western scholars. It is neither a mirror for princes nor a book of government despite the fact that it does in part talk about shahs and viziers. Notwithstanding its relative brevity, it is much more than either of those two instructional books. In its attributes it is unique to itself in the whole of classical Persian prose.

Bustan too is unique among the great treasures of classical Persian poetry. If the usual allusions to Sa'di's "practical wisdom" may be partially justified from some pages of *Golestan*, there is little if anything in *Bustan* which would justify such a description. It may be described as the theoretical and intellectual counterpart to *Golestan* to the extent that it deals with many of the themes that he has later discussed also in the latter book. But it has a wider scope and deals more closely with the ways and means of elevation and purification of the human soul. And as narrative poetry, it is one of the best Persian *mathnavis* ever written: clear, concise, fluent and readable.

Songs about human, as opposed to mystic, love could not have been written with such emotional depth and authentic feeling if the poet himself had not had a rich experience of love. However, it would clearly not follow that every *ghazal* Sa'di wrote describes or reflects an immediate concrete experience. These are written in the highest poetical diction with unsurpassed formal skill and reflect personal experiences possibly unmatched among all the Persian classical poets who wrote about the love of a fellow human being.

If by "romanticism" we refer to the philosophical and literary movement which began first in Germany in the eighteenth century and, later spreading to other European countries, reached its peak in the nineteenth century, then it would be anachronistic and irrelevant to apply it to the love songs of Sa'di and Hafiz, Rumi and the other classical Persian poets. But if the term is applied in the broader sense, reflecting mood and emotion, then Sa'di's love songs may well be compared to those of Byron, Keats, Hugo and others as part of a common human and artistic experience. There is however an English poet of the late sixteenth and early seventeenth century, some of whose love poems compare to Sa'di's in openness and audacity. This is John Donne, of the group known as the Metaphysical Poets who, later in life, combined his rich but not always happy love life with the deanship of St. Paul's Cathedral.

Sa'di was a poet and writer of the thirteenth century and one of the greatest among the Persian classical poets. His place as one of the classics is therefore secure and universal in time and space. His *Golestan* and *Bustan* contain much about timeless good and bad life that makes them relevant to any time and place where questions about moral beliefs, personal conduct and social behaviour make up an important part of the intellectual discourse. And he will always touch deeply any lover who reads his love poetry.

ENDNOTES

1 See further, Homa Katouzian, "Risheh-ha-ye Sa'di-koshi," *Iranshenasi* autumn 2002; *Sadeq Hedayat: The Life and Legend of an Iranian Writer*, paperback edition, London and New York: I. B. Tauris, 2002, chapter 1.

2 For an elaborate account and discussion, see Katouzian, "Risheh-ha-ye Sa'di-koshi."

3 See the proceedings of the conference: Habib Yaghma'i (ed), *Sa'di Nameh*, Tehran: Ministry of Education, 1938.

4 See further, Homa Katouzian, "Kasravi on Literature," *Iran Nameh*, special issue on Ahmad Kasravi, spring and summer 2002, reprinted in *Hasht Magaleh dar Tarikh va Adab-e Mo'aser*, Tehran: Nashr-e Markaz, 2006.

5 See Katouzian, "Risheh-ha-ye Sa'di-koshi."

6 See John D. Yohannan, *The Poet Sa'di, A Persian Humanist*, Boston: Bibliotheca Persica and University Press of America, 1987.

7 See this book's Selected Bibliography.

8 See ibid.

9 See Mohammad Khaza'eli, *Sharh-e Golestan*, and Henri Massé, *Essai sur le Poète Saadi*.

10 For an account of the two Jawzis see Abbas Eqbal-e Ashtiyani, "Zaman-e Tavallod va Avayel-e Zendegi-ye Sa'di' in Habib Yaghma'i (ed), *Sa'di Nameh*, Tehran: Ministry of Education, 1938.

11 For an extended discussion, see Homa Katouzian, "Safar-ha va Hazar-ha-ye Sa'di, Sa'di's Travels, 1," *Iranshenasi*, autumn 2001, and "Mara dar Nezamiyeh Edrar Bud: Sa'di's Travels, 2," *Iranshenasi*, winter 2001.

12 See Mohammad Ali Forughi (ed.), *Kolliyat-e Sa'di* (rearranged by Baha al-Din Khorramshahi), Tehran: Nashr-e Arvin, 1995, p. 755.

13 See Mohammad Khaza'eli, *Sharh-e Golestan*, Tehran, n.p., 1969; Henri Massé, *Essai sur le Poète Saadi*, Paris; Paul Geutner, 1919; and John Andrew Boyle, "The Chronology of Sa'di's Years of Travel" in R. Gramlich (ed.) *Islamwissenschaftliche Abhahdlugen Friz Meier 3am Sachzigsten Geburstag*, Weisbaden, 1974.

14 See Katuzian "Safar-ha va Hazar-ha-ye Sa'di, Sa'di's Travels, 1," *Iranshenasi*, autumn 2001, and "Mara dar Nezamiyeh Edrar Bud: Sa'di's Travels, 2," *Iranshenasi*, winter 2001.

15 *Kolliyat*, pp. 75–76.

16 *Kolliat*, pp. 87–88.

17 See further, Homa Katouzian "Farar-e Sa'di az Madreseh?," *Iranshenasi*, spring 2001.

18 *Kolliyat*, pp. 301–303.

19 *Kolliyat*, pp. 164–170. See further Homa Katouzian, "Jadal-ha-ye Sa'di," *Iranshenasi*, autumn 2000.

20 See further, Homa Katouzian, "Dorugh-e Maslahat-amiz-e Sa'di," *Iranshenasi*, summer 2002.

21 See further, Homa Katouzian, "Hemaseh-sara'i-ye Sa'di'?," *Iranshenasi*, winter 2002.

22 *Kolliyat*, pp. 31–33.

23 See further, Homa Katouzian, "*Golestan* va Afsordegi-ye Sa'di?," *Iranshenasi*, summer 2001.

24 See: Sir Lucas White King, Badayi, *The Odes of Sheikh Muslihud-Din Sa'di of Shiraz*, edited and translated with an introduction by R. A. Nicholson, Berlin: Kaviani Art Printing Press, 1925.

25 See: Rashid Yasemi in Habib Yaghma'i (ed), *Sa'di Nameh*, Tehran: Ministry of Education, 1938.

26 *Kolliyat*, p. 359.

27 For an extensive discussion of Sa'di's love poetry, see Homa Katouzian, "Sa'di dar Shab-e Hejr" *Iranshenasi*, spring, 2006. "Sa'di dar Shab-e Vasl," *Iranshenasi*, winter, 2006. "Vojuh-e Ghazal-e Sa'di," 2, *Iranshenasi*, autumn, 2005 "Vojuh-e Ghazal-e Sa'di," 1, *Iranshenasi*, summer, 2005. "Ghazale Sa'di," *Iranshenasi*, spring, 2005. "Asheqi-ha-ye Sa'di," *Iranshenasi*, winter, 2005.

28 This chapter is a revised and extended version of the following article: "Sufism in Sa'di, and Sa'di on Sufism" in Leonard Lewisohn (ed.) The *Legacy of Medieval Persian Sufism*, London and New York: Khaneqahi Nimatullahi Publications, 1992.

29 See Reuben Levy, *Persian Literature, an Introduction*, London: Oxford University Press, 1923, p. 60.

30 Ibid, p. 61.

31 See Reuben Levy, *An Introduction to Persian Literature*, New York: Columbia University Press, 1969. p. 116.

32 Ibid., p. 117.

33 Ibid.

34 See Jan Rypka, *History of Iranian Literature*, Dordrecht Holland: D. Rydal Publishing Company, 1968, p. 251.

35 See E. G. Browne, *A Literary History of Persia*, Vol. II, Cambridge: Cambridge University Press, 1923, p. 532.

36 See Annemarie Schimmel, "The Genius of Shiraz: Sa'di and Hafiz" in Ehasan Yarshater (ed.) *Persian Literature*, New York: The Persian Language Foundation, 1988, pp.214-215.

37 See Badi' al-Zaman Foruzanfar, "Sa'di va Sohravardi" in Habib Yaghma'i (ed.)

Sa'di Nameh, Tehran: Ministry of Education, 1938.

38 See Zabihollah Safa, *Tarikh-e Adabiyat dar Iran,* Vol. III, Tehran: Tehran University Press, 1974, part 1, pp. 594–595.

39 See Rashid Yasemi, "Sa'di va Eshq" in Yaghma'i (ed.) *Sa'di Nameh.*

40 See Ali Dashti, *Qalamro-ve Sa'di,* Tehran: Keyhan, 1959.

41 See Ehsan Yarshater, "The Development of Persian Literatures," in Ehsan Yarshater (ed.) *Persian Literature,* p. 26.

42 *Kolliyat,* p. 96.

43 *Kolliyat,* p. 84.

44 See for details, Homa Katouzian, "Man Estadeh-am ta Besuzam Tamam: Mysticism in Sa'di, 1," *Iranshenasi,* summer, 2003.

45 For a more extensive discussion of Sa'di on mysticism see Homa Katouzian, "Man Estadeh-am ta Besuzam Tamam: Mysticism in Sa'di, 1," and "Dar Akhlaq-e Darvishan: Mysticism in Sa'di , 2," *Iranshenasi,* winter 2004.

46 See for example, Isaiah Berlin, *The crooked timber of humanity : chapters in the history of ideas,* edited by Henry Hardy, London : John Murray, 1990.

47 *Kolliyat,* p. 157.

48 *Kolliyat,* pp. 172–186. See further, Homa Katouzian, "Baran keh dar Letafat-e Tab'ash Khalaf Nist…": Sa'di on Education, *Iranshenasi,* autumn, 2004.

49 *Kolliyat,* pp. 268–269.

50 See for example, John D. Yohannan, *The Poet Sa'di, A Persian Humanist,* Boston: Bibliotheca Persica and University Press of America, 1987.

51 *Kolliyat,* pp. 255–256.

52 *Kolliyat,* p. 77.

53 *Kolliyat,* pp. 919–921.

54 *Kolliyat,* pp. 917–919.

55 For a detailed discussion and analysis of the sociology of Iranian history see Homa Katouzian, *Iranian History and Politics,* London and New York: RoutledgeCurzon, 2003.

56 *Kolliyat,* p. 50.

57 See further, Homa Katouzian, *Iranian History and Politics,* London and New York: RoutledgeCurzon, 2003.

SELECTED BIBLIOGRAPHY

SA'DI'S WORKS IN PERSIAN

Mohammad Ali Forughi (ed.), *Kolliyat-e Sa'di*, Tehran: Amir Kabir, second edition, 1977.

Mohammad Ali Forughi (ed.), *Kolliyat-e Sa'di* (rearranged by Baha al-Din Khorramshahi) Tehran: Nashr-e Arvin, 1995.

Gholamhossein Yusefi, (ed.), *Golestan-e Sa'di,* Tehran: Kharazmi, 1987.

Gholamhossein Yusefi, (ed.), *Bustan-e Sa'di,* Tehran: Kharazmi, 2002.

Mohammad Khaza'eli, *Sharh-e Bustan*, Tehran: Javidan, n.d.

Mohammad Khaza'eli, *Sharh-e Golestan*, Tehran, n.p., 1969.

Mirza Ebrahim and Mirza Karim Mozaffri (eds), *Kollyat-e Sa'di*, Bombay: Mozaffari, 1917.

SA'DI'S WORKS IN EUROPEAN LANGUAGES

R. M. Alieva, *Gulistan, Kriticheskii Tekst Predislovie I Primechaniia*, Moskva : Izdatel'stvo vostochnoi literatury, 1959.

A. J. Arberry, *Kings and Beggars*, London: Luzac&Co., 1945.

E. Arnold, Sir, *The Gulistan, Being the Rose-Garden of Shaikh Sadi, the first four Babs, or "Gateways,"* London, 1899.

—— *With Sa'di in the Garden; or, The book of love, the 3rd chapter of the "Bôstân,"* London, 1888.

K. Chaykin, *Bustan*, Moscow, 1935.

L. Cranmer-Byng, *The Rose-Garden of Sa'di, Selected and Rendered with Introduction*, London: J. Murray, 1905.

Andrè Du Ryer, *Gulistan ou L'Empire des Roses*, Paris, 1634.

Edward Eastwick, *The Rose-Garden of Sheikh Muslihu'd-din Sa'di of Shiraz*, London: Octagon Press, 1974.

Georgius Gentius, *Musladin Sadi Rosarium Politicum, sive Amoenum Sortis Humanae Theatrum in Lat. versum, Necessariisque Notis Illustr. A G. Gentio*, Amsterdam, 1651.

Francis Gladwin, *The Gulistan or Rose-Garden by Muslehuddeen Shaikh Sâdy of Sheeraz*, London; Kingsbury, Parbury and Allen, 1822.

Lucas White King, Sir, *Badayi, The Odes of Sheikh Muslihud-Din Sa'di of Shiraz, edited and Translated with an introduction by R. A. Nicholson*, Berlin: Kaviani Art Printing Press, 1925.

—— *Tayyibat : the Odes of Sheikh Muslihu'd-Din Sad'i Shirazi / translated by the late Sir Lucas White King, with an introduction by Reynold A. Nicholson*, London: Luzac&Co, 1926.

Reuben Levy, *Stories form the Bustan of Sheikh Sa'di*, London: Chapman and Hall, 1928.

C. A. Barbier de Meynard, *Le Boustan ou Verger*, Paris: Ernest Leroux, 1880.

Adam Olearius, *Persianischer Rosenthal, von A. Oleario in hochdeutscher Sprache mit historien, notis vnd figuren vermehret vnd verbessert heraus gegeben*, Schlesswig, 1660.

John Platts, *The Gulistan of Shaikh Muslihu'd Din Sa'di of Shiraz*, London: Kegan Paul, Trench, Trubner &Co., 1874

Edward Rehatsek, *Persian and English Gulistan*, Tehran, 1988.

James Ross, *The Gulistan or Flower Garden of Shaikh Sa'di of Shiraz*, London: J. M. Robinson, 1823.

Friedrich Rückert, *Sa'di's Bostan*, Leipzig: S. Hirzel, 1882.

Sa'di, *L'argento di un povero cuore : centouno ghazal di Sa'di Shir°azi / a cura di Setrag Manoukian*, Rome : Instituto culturale della repubblica islamica dell'Iran in Italia, 1991(selected poems, Italian and Persian).

—— *Select Fables from Gulistan or the Bed of Roses, Translated from the original Persian of Sa'di*, London, 1773.

Charles Sayle, *Gulistan or Flower-Garden, Sadi*, London: Walter Scott, 1890.

Arthur Scholey, *The Discontented Dervishes and other Persian Tales, Retold from Sa'di*; illustrated by William Rushton, London: Deutsch, 1977.

Stephen Sullivan Esq., *Select Fables from Gulistan or the Bed of Roses, Translated from the Original Persian of Sa'di*, London: J. Ridley, 1774.

G. M. Wickens, *The Bustan of Sa'di*, J. A. Brill: Leiden, 1974

CRITICAL STUDIES

A.J. Arberry, *Classical Persian Literature,* Oxford: Clarendon Press, 1958.

— (ed.), *The Legacy of Persia*, Oxford: Clarendon Press, 1953.

John Andrew Boyle, "The Chronology of Sa'di's Years of Travel" in R. Gramlich (ed.) *Islamwissenschaftliche AbhahdlugenFriz Meier 3am Sachzigsten Geburstag*, Weisbaden, 1974.

Edward G. Browne, *A Literary History of Persia*, Vol. II, Cambridge: Cambridge University Press, 1923.

Ali Dashti, *Qalmro-e, Sa'di*, Tehran: Keyhan, 1959.

Abbas Eqbal-e Ashtiyani, 'Zaman-e Tavallod va Avayel-e Zendegi-ye Sa'di' in Habib Yaghma'i (ed), *Sa'di Nameh*, Tehran: Ministry of Education, 1938.

Homa Katouzian, "Sufism in Sa'di, and Sa'di on Sufism" in Leonard Lewisohn (ed.), The *Legacy of Medieval Persian Sufism*, London and New York: Khaneqahi Nimatullahi Publications, 1992.

— "Jadal-ha-ye Sa'di," *Iranshenasi, autumn* 2000.

— "Farar-e Sa'di az Madreseh?," *Iranshenasi*, spring 2001.

— "*Golestan* va Afsordegi-ye Sa'di?," *Iranshenasi*, summer 2001.

— "Safar-ha va Hazar-ha-ye Sa'di, Sa'di's Travels, 1," *Iranshenasi*, autumn 2001.

— "Mara dar Nezamiyeh Edrar Bud': Sa'di's Travels, 2," *Iranshenasi*, winter 2001.

— *Sadeq Hedayat: The Life and Legend of an Iranian Writer*, paperback edition, London and New York: I. B. Tauris, 2002.

— "Kasravi on Literature," *Iran Nameh,* special issue on Ahmad Kasravi, spring and summer 2002.

— "Dorugh-e Maslahat-amiz-e Sa'di," *Iranshenasi*, summer 2002.

— "Risheh-ha-ye Sa'di-koshi," *Iranshenasi* autumn 2002.

— "Hemaseh-sara'i-ye Sa'di?," *Iranshenasi*, winter 2002.

— *Iranian History and Politics*, London and New York: RoutledgeCurzon, 2003.

— "Man Estadeh-am ta Besuzam Tamam: Mysticism in Sa'di, 1," *Iranshenasi*, summer, 2003.

— "Sa'di va Padshahan," *Iranshenasi*, spring 2004.

— "Sa'di va Vaziran," *Iranshenasi*, summer, 2004

—— "Baran keh dar Letafat-e Tab'ash Khalaf Nist…": Sa'di on Education, *Iranshenasi*, autumn, 2004.

—— "Dar Akhlaq-e Darvishan: Mysticism in Sa'di , 2," *Iranshenasi*, winter 2005.

—— "Ghazal-e Sa'di," *Iranshenasi*, spring, 2005.

—— "Vojuh-e Ghazal-e Sa'di," 1, *Iranshenasi*, summer, 2005.

—— "Vojuh-e Ghazal-e Sa'di," 2, *Iranshenasi*, autumn, 2005.

—— "Asheqi-ha-ye Sa'di," *Iranshenasi*, winter, 2005.

—— "Sa'di dar Shab-e Hejr" *Iranshenasi*, spring, 2006.

—— "Sa'di dar Shab-e Vasl," *Iranshenasi*, winter, 2006.

Ruben Levy, *Persian literature, An Introduction*, London: Oxford University Press, 1923.

—— *An Introduction to Persian Literature*, New York: Columbia University Press, 1969.

Henri Massé, *Essai sur le Poète Saadi*, Paris; Paul Geutner, 1919.

—— *Tahqiq darbareh-ye Sa'di*, Gholamhossein Yusefi and Mohammad Hasan Mahdavi Ardebili (trs.) Tehran: Tus, 1970.

Sa'id Nafisi, "Tarikh-e Dorost-e Dargozasht-e Sa'di," *Mjalleh-ye Daneshkadeh-ye Adabiyat-e Tehran*, 1958.

Jan Rypka, *History of Iranian Literature*, Dordrecht Holland: D. Rydal Publishing Company, 1968.

Zabihollah Safa, *Tarikh-e Adabiyyat dar Iran*, Vol. III, Tehran: Tehran University Press, 1974.

Annemarie Schimmel, "The Genius of Shiraz: Sa'di and Hafez" in Ehsan Yarshater (ed.) *Persian Literature*: Albany, N.Y.: Bibliotheca Persica, 1988.

Habib Yaghma'i (ed.), *Sa'di Nameh*, Tehran: Ministry of Education, 1938.

Ehsan Yarshater, "The Development of Persian Literatures," in Ehsan Yarshater (ed.) *Persian Literature*.

John D. Yohannan, *The Poet Sa'di, A Persian Humanist*, Boston: Bibliotheca Persica and University Press of America, 1987.

INDEX